"*Bones & Honey* is a book of portals, each one opening to ancient ways of remembrance and reclamation. The old ways of storytelling live on in these pages, offering medicine for wild hearts. Beautifully woven through prayers, spells, and stories, Danielle Dulsky's words speak straight to the beating heart of the human experience, in all its timeless expressions."

— **Celeste Larsen**, author of *Heal the Witch Wound: Reclaim Your Magic and Step into Your Power*

"In *Bones & Honey*, Danielle Dulsky artfully combines poetic allure with ancient insights, creating a narrative that profoundly touches the contemporary heart. Each page brims with nature-inspired prayers, mythic chants, and tales that rekindle our innate bond to the universe around us. Through her evocative prose, Danielle not only reshapes our understanding of prayer for today's world but also reignites the age-old connection between the reader and the natural realm. Her words stand as both a sanctuary and a revelation, bearing testament to the tenacity and grace of the human spirit and offering solace to those wearied by the tumult of modern existence. Danielle's deep reverence for the natural and the ethereal radiates throughout, drawing readers into a realm where they can reconnect with the rhythms of a time long past yet ever present. As a guiding light for mindful existence, *Bones & Honey* encourages readers to delve deep, immerse themselves, and let Danielle's transformative writings rejuvenate their souls. The book stands as a balm in our chaotic era, championing a return to unhurried, thoughtful living and a renewed appreciation for the enchantment that is woven through our lives. Each chapter, centered around evocative archetypes, crafts a vision of hope, resilience, and the timeless power of our bond with the cosmos. In a world on the edge, Danielle presents a haven of words and wisdom, a realm where souls can find comfort and inspiration."

— **Mat Auryn**, bestselling author of *Psychic Witch*, *Mastering Magick*, and *Pisces Witch*

"Danielle Dulsky is one of the most embodied truth sayers I have the pleasure of knowing. Her latest offering, *Bones & Honey*, gifts readers with another masterfully crafted, visceral, and hauntingly beautiful book. The prose is equal parts eloquent, illumined, and inspiring and will stay with the reader long after they've turned the last page. Thank you, Danielle, for this wonderfully heathenistic gift to the world."

— **Chris Grosso**, author of *Indie Spiritualist* and *Necessary Death*

"Danielle Dulsky's book *Bones & Honey* offers us a deeper place to go when we need a deeper kind of prayer, the kind that speaks light into darkness and primal breath into death. She gives us stories to set ourselves in, to see ourselves in, and inspires us to continue on our rose-and-thorns paths. This is a book that we can come back to time and time again when we're feeling lost and need the guidance of the moonlight."

— **Ora North**, author of *Mood Magick* and *I Don't Want to Be an Empath Anymore*

# BONES

## &

# HONEY

## Also by Danielle Dulsky

*Woman Most Wild: Three Keys to Liberating the Witch Within*

*The Holy Wild: A Heathen Bible for the Untamed Woman*

*Seasons of Moon and Flame:*
*The Wild Dreamer's Epic Journey of Becoming*

*Sacred Hags Oracle: Visionary Guidance for Dreamers, Witches,*
*and Wild Hearts* (with illustrations by Janine Houseman)

*The Holy Wild Grimoire:*
*A Heathen Handbook of Magick, Spells, and Verses*

# BONES
## &
# HONEY

*A Heathen Prayer Book*

# DANIELLE DULSKY

New World Library
Novato, California

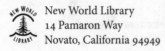

New World Library
14 Pamaron Way
Novato, California 94949

An early version of the text found on pages 29–30, 102–4, and 118–19 has appeared on the website *The House of Twigs*.

Text design by Megan Colman. Typography by Tona Pearce Myers.

Library of Congress Cataloging-in-Publication data is available.

First printing, November 2023
ISBN 978-1-60868-892-0
Ebook ISBN 978-1-60868-893-7
Printed in Canada on 100% postconsumer-waste recycled paper

New World Library is proud to be a Gold Certified Environmentally Responsible Publisher. Publisher certification awarded by Green Press Initiative.

10  9  8  7  6  5  4  3  2  1

*To the white wolf*

# CONTENTS

## 2. The Book of Wild Lovers: Prayers for Lust, Seduction, and Majestic Relatedness

## 4. The Book of the Heathen Queen: Prayers for Empowerment, Sovereignty, and Truth Telling      55

## 5. The Book of the Moon: Prayers for Secret Keepers, Midnight Poets, and Fringe Dwellers      63

## 6. The Book of the Mountain Mage: Prayers for Sacred Solitude, Transformation, and Inner Alchemy    83

## 7. The Book of the Wounded Healer: Prayers for Heartache, Healing, and the Shining Self    89

## 11. The Book of the Shepherd: Prayers for Nurturing, Self-Love, and Space Tending

## 12. The Book of Shape-Shifters: Prayers for Time Weavers, Human Evolution, and Strange Futures

# THE TRICKSTER'S BONE BROTH

## *An Introduction*

*Every morning is a heathen morning.* Upon waking, just before time's crust thickens around our vision, we are all ageless wanderers haunting those wild brambles that border the dreamlands. Here, we wear a cloak hand-stitched from crow feathers and snakeskin, swaying to the sound of wolf song and listening deeply to otherworldly voices. Here, on this untamed ground, we are a nameless ancestor dancing at the overgrown crossroads between the dreaming self and the doing self, and just here, we are offered our daily libation by the trickster's hand.

If we choose, we might all wake sipping a strange elixir these days, an apocalyptic bone broth of wonder, anticipation, and generative befuddlement, spiced with a peppery dash of righteous rage and sweetened with a honeyed spoonful of innocence. If we drink with care, if we savor the splendid brew offered us by the edge dweller, we find ourselves at home in a shape-shifting world where, suddenly and against all odds, nothing is impossible. To be heathen, after all, is to live on uncultivated ground, and to be alive today is to be an apprentice midwife in the birthing room for a wilder world.

Many who chose to be born here and now, during this volatile chapter in the world story, harbor the wily soul of the trickster; they prefer to live on the fringes, where that timely medicine called awe is at its most potent, where truth is better felt in the body than seen on a screen, and where prayers are sung by those poet-tongued heathens who remember why they came to visit this time and place. The trickster knows that the best plans are seeded in dreams and measured in generations, and if we let our inner edge dweller speak, their words just might sting us into an aliveness more exquisite than we have ever known.

## Prayers of the Seer-Innocents

Uncertainty has the power to invite innocence or arrogance, and these are shadow-filled times indeed. If we choose innocence — if we allow the rough, frozen edges around what we believe to be true to thaw and soften just a bit — we might dare to name ourselves a seer. A seer walks with one foot in the Otherworld. A seer is half child and half hag, a soothsayer who holds the long-vision, who will not be stunned by crisis, who embodies both the splendid wisdom of elderhood and the tender curiosity of a babe.

The old seers' prayers match the prayers of the innocents, intricately woven songs for all beings to be free, midnight petitions to unnamed gods for every earthly creature to sense they belong to something far greater than any one, individual story. These prayers are hummed and howled in moments of solitude, whispered into the bathroom mirror, sung at the threshold of a mausoleum, danced on a holy hilltop, and wept over the kitchen sink. These prayers of the seer-innocents are spontaneous verses of gratitude and grief, echoes of an older-than-ancient knowing that, below the concrete, something wild stirs awake.

## Timely Word Stories

Every word contains a story, a story that began centuries ago, a story that continues to unfold even now. The etymology of *apocalypse*, for instance, is derived from a root meaning "to reveal" or "to lift the veil." In these times of climate collapse, the vast curtain on the world stage, once the temporary backdrop for a human-centric drama, is rising to reveal a more-than-human play far more complex than even we, the freaks, might have imagined. We were busy watching the haggard kings battle the everymen and forgot about the cunning fox-women, immortal children, and bone-witches. As the curtain continues to rise, more people are finding a home in the old stories where magick is always afoot, where archetypes are small gods who speak the language of myth. If we listen, just maybe, these archetypes might orient us toward the greatest version of ourselves and, by extension, the most wondrous version of this world.

The etymology of *archetype* goes back to the Greek meaning "original form." Archetypes are once-and-future blueprints, bone-and-stone maps of the mythic psyche. When certain archetypes are shrouded and ignored, our own stories and the world story unfold accordingly, without the monologues of wounded healers and warrior-shepherds, the spotlight shining on the familiar faces of sick kings and their soldiers. When lost archetypes are again revealed and brought forth, the world story is renewed.

To lift the veil is to welcome new possibilities to take center stage, to move, challenge, and confuse us into action, and here is where we find ourselves now, with a curtain half-raised to reveal the shadows and strange footsteps of these new-old forms, these new-old thespians. The word-story origin of *thespian* is "inspired by the gods." Our timely task is to not merely witness this wild drama but to consciously join it, to disturb the familiar plot and take our meaningful place on the stage among the mages and shape-shifters while acknowledging that, in the end, every character holds a piece of our own wholeness, a fragment of our own "original form" that was, after all, "inspired by the gods," the gods before there were gods.

## Heathen Prayers for Modernity's Wilder Children

The universal human quest to name ourselves whole seems to drive the plotline of any personal myth. We seek to recover what has been lost in ourselves and, by extension, in the world. This age-old quest requires battle and, strangely, both victory and defeat. We know this story well;

we learn this story as children, meeting it over and over again in film and literature until it seems to be the only story worth telling. All the while, we sense there is a hidden undercurrent of magick belowground, a subterranean story far wilder than what we see play out on the battle-fields, where armored heroes still reign supreme, a heathen story whis-pered into being each day by us, the Witches, the tricksters, and the healers, those of us who have few prayer books written for us, those who dwell on the fringes of every story and just might call the Earth and her wildest imaginings our god.

In this book, you will find a peculiar collection of prayers, blessings, songs, and small stories for the heathen-hearted, for modernity's unruly children. The word *prayer*, from the Old French for "earnest request," implies a solemnity the churchless tend to shun, reawakening child-hood memories of kneeling before a male savior. The word *heathen* may evoke Pagan images of blood sacrifice and hidden rituals held in dark forests, but the word story reveals a deeper origin; heathens were "dwellers on the heath," those who lived in rural areas, the last to be Christianized and colonized. As the veil continues to lift, as the curtain rises to reveal far more sacred actors than the few famed gods whose names we all know well, we still need prayer. We have our own "earnest requests," not for forgiveness or redemption but for all beings, ourselves included, to be whole, well, and free.

Our heathen prayers hold no desperation. Such petitions, much like a spell, are not sourced from defeat but desire, rooted in a deep understanding that the next chapter in the world story will have many nonhuman authors, and to be in communion with these creaturely, el-emental, and otherworldly scribes is to — consciously, sensuously, and emphatically — take part in the story's grand unfolding. There is a vi-tality to prayer. There is an undeniable heat to words spoken with in-tention. Prayer troubles us into participation, disturbing even our best illusions of humanity's separateness from what is sacred and unseen. To pray is not to submit but to cast a spell, to speak our imaginations aloud and make manifest our most earnest requests. No spell comes to fruition without the confluence of innumerable forces, and every Witch knows this well. By extension, every spell is, in part, a prayer.

Explore this heathen prayer book as you would wander through those borderlands on the edge of dreaming, trusting you will find the precise vision the deep soul needs. There is no need to read linearly; your inner trickster would not want you to. You might ask yourself which of the thirteen books calls to you the loudest and begin there:

### 1. *The Book of Stars*
#### Prayers for Hope's Troublemakers, Impossible Freaks, and Stubborn Visionaries

Written in defense of hope, the thirteen prayers in The Book of Stars are spoken by our inner visionary, the one who holds the long-vision and finds a perplexing joy in imagining strange futures. We find medicine in the visionary's prayers when our stubborn hope feels lonely, when our fellow dreamers are few.

### 2. *The Book of Wild Lovers*
#### Prayers for Lust, Seduction, and Majestic Relatedness

The chalice of our inner lover runs over with worldly lust. The Book of Wild Lovers holds thirteen prayers written by the one who sees beauty in all things, who seduces the world into being one mud-and-moss love song at a time. We find medicine in our inner lover's prayers when we witness the sensuality of a woodland snowfall or our passion is ignited by the scent of the sea, when we find ourselves swollen with eco-lust and a holy ache to be licked alive by the rain.

### 3. *The Book of the Bone-Witch*
#### Prayers for Grievers, Death Walkers, and Shadow Kin

The thirteen prayers in The Book of the Bone-Witch are mourned aloud by our inner death walker, the part of us who speaks the language of grief and holds the tension of the dying times. We find a gift in her keening songs when we sense part of our world lies dying, in those initiatory moments when only sorrow makes sense and darkness somehow brings a great and terrible comfort.

### 4. The Book of the Heathen Queen
Prayers for Empowerment, Sovereignty, and Truth Telling

Our inner royal might erect walls around our heart or hinder the free-doms enjoyed by our more rebellious parts, but we also harbor an inner heathen queen, an untamed ruler who wishes to protect our wildness above all things. Her prayers are for truth. Her prayers are to feel sover-eign within the collective, to find the strangest possibilities imaginable and name them law for a time. We find medicine in her prayers, the thirteen prayers in The Book of the Heathen Queen, when fear lurks behind the standing stones of our most heathen ways, when we require orders from our inner ruler to stand our ground.

### 5. The Book of the Moon
Prayers for Secret Keepers, Midnight Poets, and Fringe Dwellers

Within The Book of the Moon, we find thirteen prayers whisper-hissed by the inner trickster, the shadow fox who dwells at the crossroads of our dreamlands. The elixir of the trickster is not easily digested, and their prayers are for deep and deranged transformation. We find medi-cine in the trickster's prayers when a plot twist in our story or the world story shocks us awake and disrupts our best laid plans.

### 6. The Book of the Mountain Mage
Prayers for Sacred Solitude, Transformation, and Inner Alchemy

The mountain mage speaks the alchemical language of change born of will. The mage finds magick in the storm and meaning in chaos. The thirteen prayers of the mage are for empowerment, for the spark of inner vitality that feeds us all. We find medicine in the mage's prayers when our world falls into a sepia-toned monotony, when our own magick feels elusive and the voice of the Otherworld falls silent.

### 7. The Book of the Wounded Healer
Prayers for Heartache, Healing, and the Shining Self

The wounded healer limps through the world carrying the most potent medicine for these times. The thirteen prayers of the wounded healer are spoken and sung from the soul's underworld, prayers for all to find meaning in their woundedness and healing through their souls' unique, innate gift. We require the prayers of the wounded healer when our hidden treasures are about to be witnessed by the world, when the old wound begins to bleed at precisely the moment when our inner shining one starts singing.

### 8. The Book of the Nameless Grandmothers
#### Prayers for Ancestral Healing, Lineage Exploration, and Forgiveness

In The Book of the Nameless Grandmothers, we find thirteen prayers by the inner crone's hand, the aged and wise part of ourselves who has seen such apocalyptic times before, who knows how this story will end. We find medicine in the crone's prayers when the wounds of our lineage ache, when our story gets nipped by rootlessness and that ancestral longing to belong.

### 9. The Book of the Pagan Warrioress
#### Prayers for Battle, Bone Gathering, and Beauty

Our inner warrioress understands the etymology of the word *war*, from the old Germanic for "to confuse." Her prayers are for the courage to hone her innermost genius, to acquire the skills needed to enact her purpose and "confuse" the world she wants to see birthed into being. We name the warrioress's prayers, the thirteen prayers in The Book of the Pagan Warrioress, as our medicine when the old fights are insufficient, when victory feels elusive and all our weapons are dull and broken.

### 10. The Book of the Botanical Babe
#### Prayers for Innocents, Beginnings, and Wild Children

The thirteen prayers in The Book of the Botanical Babe speak to our inner innocent, to the wide-eyed babe who sits behind our fear. The prayers of the innocent are prayers to see the world in ways unshaped by the embittered patterns of experience, to consider that there may be an undiscovered heirloom seed left buried in even the rockiest, overtilled soil. We find medicine in the innocent's prayers when rebirth feels elusive, when we begin the renewal stage of an initiation and blink awake as if for the first time.

### 11. The Book of the Shepherd
Prayers for Nurturing, Self-Love, and Space Tending

Deep within The Book of the Shepherd dreams our inner nurturer, the soft-spoken one who is concerned with care of the self, other, and the world. The thirteen prayers of our inner caregiver are prayers to tend to the soul, to put down the sword and pick up a spoon. We find medicine in the nurturer's prayers when our fires have burned too hot for too long, when our most productive wells are running dry; in these times, our inner shepherdess calls her flock home to graze under the stars for a time.

### 12. The Book of Shape-Shifters
Prayers for Time Weavers, Human Evolution, and Strange Futures

The shape-shifter prays to the yet-to-be self, to the one who has already evolved into a form that lives closer to what they love. Our inner shape-shifter has befriended our creaturely nature, our inner uncivilized one who is more wild than modern, who keeps their pelt close. The shape-shifter's prayers, the thirteen prayers in The Book of Shape-Shifters, are medicine when we question the merit of convenience, when our heathen skin is our greatest treasure and all else is illusion.

### 13. The Book of Bones and Honey
Prayers for the Bittersweetness of a Most Heathen Life

In the most cataclysmic moments in the world story, new characters are birthed, unrecognizable archetypes who wander onto the stage to teach us something about the next act. The Book of Bones and Honey contains thirteen prayers written for the bittersweetness of this life, for the strangest part of our soul that, for reasons that can never be fully known to us until we cross death's threshold, chose to be here for this apocalyptic moment in time. Bones are what remain when all else burns away, at once terrible reminders of life's impermanence and universal symbols of what endures. Honey is sweet, earthly medicine, a gift from the hive and a living reflection of our endangered kinship to the untamed lands. Bones are a promise that something lives on after death, and honey calls us to tend to the sweetness of life.

My prayer, my "earnest request," is for you to find a hidden home somewhere in these pages. May a ghostly phrase or peculiar word haunt you in just the right places, and may you call it your new, secret name. Know those words as a sacred spell emblazoned upon the red and thumping skin of your heart-drum, kept quiet and close until you find yourself among the most soulful thespian-poets on the world stage as the curtain finally rises, howling those words into the shadows and bidding them become the first epic line in a new, wilder-than-human drama.

And so it is.

# 1

# THE BOOK OF STARS

*Prayers for Hope's Troublemakers,
Impossible Freaks, and Stubborn Visionaries*

*Dire times are marked by the guilt* of the visionaries. Those who stubbornly dream of a world they might call *better* — who can see something luminous eventually rising from these ruins, who feel a strange sense of joy when an old system begins to crumble — often tuck these brighter visions away for fear of being seen as naive, over-privileged, sheltered, woundless, or secretly masking shadow with light. They hush their hope. They hide their impossibly possible visions, lock-ing their inner visionary inside the highest tower of their psychic house, where they can see for a hundred million miles, for a hundred million years. Here, they dream in silence.

Our inner visionary is the part of us who understands the urgency of these times, who holds the tension between hope and hopelessness and, even now, sees a story that is just beginning, an amber-gold inkling of dawn on a dark horizon. The eyes of the visionary can see into the deep future and deep past, finding themselves full of faith that all time is happening at once. They are stunned into silence by the splendor of what endures, the spiral dance of galaxies and the miraculous fusion of stars. They are bitten to life by the aching beauty of the world, and their prayers are for renewal, for revolution and evolution.

The archetype of the visionary is not built from endless optimism, boundless innovative ideas, and relentless cheer. Most often the life of the visionary is lonely. To live as the visionary lives is to wake with an unwavering trust that the sun will rise but still finding the clock stopped at the edge of dawn.

The prayers in this Book of Stars are prayers for meaning, prayers to soothe the soul that hopes too much. Imagine your inner visionary, that part of you who still holds faith for the world's bettering, standing before an open window in a tall tower. Their eyes are wide open, and from here they see it all; they see the plastic islands, famines, and melting ice caps, and they see re-wilded fields, thriving children, and radical art. They look to the east, speaking these words to a vast indigo sky full of stars, whispering to a slow-rising sun only they can see. These prayers are their prayers and yours.

## 1.1. Temples of Moss, Lichen, and Stone
### *An Anthem for the Churchless*

The visionary can raise a temple at the river's edge. They can build a cathedral from shells and name a fallen tree their shrine. This prayer is for the times when a peculiar holiness wants to be marked, when small and solitary ritual is the most necessary medicine.

A nameless ceremony is afoot, this troubled dawn. An echo of an old heathen memory is rattling through the caverns of my modern mind, and I'm raising a hood woven from snakeskin, frost-flecked moss, last year's orphaned dreams, and the storm-wet feathers of shape-shifting crows. I'm leaving my house and heading west, howling to the Otherworld and carrying a lone lantern to light the way. I cannot say why I must go, but I can say even the churchless need a place to pray. Even the unrepenting sinners who sip a daily nectar leached from forbidden fruit need a holy sanctuary where the trees are Priestesses and communion is taken from rainwater, mushrooms, and wild strawberries. Only here, only in my temple of moss, lichen, and stone, can I cast a sudden spell of irrational hope upon my heart. Only here, deep in the ghost-filled woodland beyond my best-built fences, can I sense the oracular songs of those long-gone-still-here ones who called the land god, who named this forest kin. To them, I say thank you.

## 1.2. A Wish for the Stubborn Dreamer
### *For Those Who Strive Even Now*

Though every visionary knows this, sometimes naming our belonging to a greater community of hopeful dreamers is crucial to our well-being, to the wholeness of our spirit. Hope is a bitter business. Visions want a witness, and this prayer is for those other seers who dream like we dream, who pray like we pray.

May you foresee a wilder way to be even now, even as the most ancient story spreads her legs to give birth to a new myth. A long labor it will surely be, but, even now, my wish is for you to be the birth song. Be wonder. Be Witch and bewitch. May you eat your shadows, befriend your inner beasts, and behold the grand poetry of this moment with black-mirror eyes hungry for visionary art and untamed truths. Be soothsayer. Be myth dweller. Seek out story medicine where a rough land is a she-king and the children become the voices of the oldest gods. Keep going. There is an art that can be made only by you and only here in this birthing room, where the mother of a beyond-human fairy tale labors long past an apocalyptic midnight. Tend this art well; let it stain your hands. Be guile and beguile. Such is my wish for you.

## 1.3. In Praise of Eternal Time
### *A Work Song for the Apocalyptic Self*

For all of us, for you, for me, there is a work song we sing to slip beyond the veil, to furl our wings and fall softly into the long-stretching spaces of eternal time. This apocalyptic hymn is shaped differently by every tongue it finds, but even so, these songs share a familiar knowing, a deep and enduring understanding that time, like space, is far vaster and wilder than our rational minds might fathom. To sense eternal time is to commune with the wiser self, to bid the trappings of the clock and calendar fall away, to hum this tune for the end of days, for the birth of days, to do the arduous work of breaking the cage of linear time around our more heathen ways. May we, the visionaries, sing this song often and well.

May I live long hours as my least civilized self, taking my rhythms from falling rain and birdsong, sipping my light from the sun and leaving behind my tamer ways. I take this next breath as if it were my last, and I howl that one thunderous word that shatters every brightly lit screen and stops every pendulum from swinging. Here, I am lost in wonder. I am a woodland creature listening deeply to the soul song of the heathen lands and mirroring the pulse of the Holy Wild with every footfall. Here, I am my most apocalyptic self, full of freedom and rich in time. And so it is.

## 1.4. Inviting the Small Voice to Sing
### *To Empower a Vision*

A slow-to-shadow moon calls a somber sky its home, this night of revelations and quickening seeds, and my mind's eye sees a vision I call my singular desire. Be a lantern lighting my path, dear moon, and invite my small voice to sing. Cast your silver-light spells on the faces of the storytelling ghosts and warmhearted mystics who know me best. Empower this vision of mine now, for I cannot wait for your fullness. When midnight finds me at the fireside blanketed in longing and bidding the clock speed forth that I might find my vision realized, remind me this: If it can be imagined, if I can behold this vision in all its glory, it is already real. On some timeline in some wild place, my vision is already unfolding. My desire is already mine, and I am already blooming with gratitude, my shining self glorified by the beauty of another dream fulfilled.

## 1.5. In Memory of the Weary Poet
### *To Mark a Difficult Moment*

Hope is a treacherous discipline, but when we create art from our hopeful visions, we find not only our human desire for yet-to-be-born generations to live well; we also find an undeniable truth. We know if we can imagine this coming dawn, then somehow, somewhere, this dawn already exists. Art makes the imagined real, always, and the poet who grows weary of the world writes to stun the impossible world into being.

To my heavy soul, tonight I pray to you. When the sun sets on my hope, I welcome that strange spirit I call witness. I bid that mist-cloaked crone take the empty seat at my side and weep with me. Together, we each shed three tears, for fate, destiny, and emergence, bidding them become a swift-running river that carries away our despair, bringing our time-less sorrow home to the great-grandmother ocean, where it might rejoin the source of all things. Here, I wish to fix nothing. Here, I remember the once-and-future poet whose words remind me human heartbreak is ancient and enduring. To be human is to find beauty in the ache, mean-ing in the melancholy, and truth be told, I believe I may be made by this moment. When healing finally finds me, may I remember the whispers I hear now in the time of my gravest sadness, for only in these depths can I hear the voice of the innocents reminding me to carry on. To the Witness, to the wild children, I say thank you.

## 1.6. The Strangest Joy
### *To Honor Our Many Contradictions*

We are full of tensions, strung together by so many opposing be-liefs and conflicting desires. Our inner complexities can never be reconciled fully by our rational minds, and tireless attempts to do so will always bring agony. Instead, the heathen befriends this truth: it's the tension between our many contradictions that empowers us, that resources us in troubled times. Our inner visionary sometimes dares to play chess with our inner naysayer, and this prayer starts the game.

Tonight, I'm building a small woodland hut in my haunted dreamscape to house my many contradictions. The story of my life is full of wise children, mountain dwellers, and those otherworldly creatures I've met along the road. Just for tonight, I'm leaving my old, gnarled fear outside the door. I'm making a bed for my wonder to rest alongside my rage, and I'm tending a fire in the hearth called paradox. Here, I vow to live in chaos and order, silence and song, sanctuary and wilderness. Here, I sleep well, full of the strangest joy. Wait for me.

## 1.7. A Song for the Death Eaters
*To Whisper When the Day Was Hard*

When we allow our inner visionaries to be witnessed and seen, we are inevitably made vulnerable to hope's critics. We get bitten by the fangs of skepticism. Only pessimists can be trusted these days, it seems, and the visionary wakes in a world that fails to match their dreams. This prayer is for the most difficult days, when the friends were few, the why-bother days that threatened to send us into our solitary caves forever.

On this, the night of all nights, I sing a honey-tongued anthem as the sun sets on a dying day full of strife and sharp words. I howl this wild dirge into the spiraling tunnels of deep time. May it disturb my bitterness and be dreamt by my older-than-ancient ancestors who have seen such days before, who hold and shield me even now when fate's thread is a tightening noose, even now as a red moon rises.

To this day I say good riddance. I say I was born for this. I can hear the once-and-future echoes of Pagan poetry whispered by the innocents, and I know I was made for these rough times that temper and shape the soul. I see the winged harbingers of death-and-rebirth circling the skies, and I bid them carry these last long hours I have lived away. Take this day to the borderlands, you foulmouthed beasts! Pull the daggers of the envious ones' words from my flesh and leave me here to heal in my sleep.

In my haunted dreamlands, surely, I will commune with a wiser version of myself who knows why this day was scripted into my story, but for now, may the ravenous raptors descend and pick clean the bones of this moment when my protectors have been few and the shadows many. Tomorrow I will wake with a new song drumming inside my heart, but for tonight, my hymn is for the death eaters, a eulogy for a day gone sour.

## 1.8. Soup from the Seer Hag
*When a Terrible Vision Comes*

A visionary sees both grief and joy on the horizon. To be a seer during these volatile times means witnessing the woundedness of humanity in all its terrible forms. This prayer is for the moments when the visionary's eyes are met by tragedy.

Ah! This seer is struck by the horror of humanity's current season, frozen into stillness by another storm in this, our longest winter. When the mightiest visions come, they come swift, steady, and sure; they are marred by old blades and steeped in new blood. When the prophecies are too terrible to speak aloud, I bid the old seer hag find me in my dreams and gift my soul with a bit of soup and song. I bid this elder tend a humble fire just for me and listen to my sharper stories of floodwaters and flames. She, this elder, and I, we wear the same amulet, I think, and I know her to be my nameless foremother. I know her to be the unburnable one, and surely I will wake held by the long arms of time, the taste of her heady brew on my tongue and the sound of her somber prophet's song echoing in the red chambers of my seer's heart. Together, we hold the madness of this moment. Together, we find meaning in the meaningless.

## 1.9. New Year's Eve
*A Song for Overzealous Visionaries*

A new year's eve need not be one that marks the end of a calendar year. Any initiatory evening might be a new year's evening, and on those nights, this is the visionary's prayer.

This new year's eve, may we weave a luminous tapestry of light, shadow, and hopeful song, as deep change haunts our waking dreams. May we crown ourselves with the bones of the old year, innocence, icicles, and frost-skinned twigs, telling ghost stories and whispering lost love poems when dusk comes early, drumming the rhythms our souls remember but our minds forgot, dancing our most prophetic prayers for the new year, for the holy, wild world.

### 1.10. Coins in the Couch
*To Whisper When the Money Is Gone*

Caught in a tireless circus I never cared to join, I am. Tonight, I dig for coins in the couch and name my many riches. May my unseen protectors come close and warm the cold bones of my house. May they hear my songs while I pull dollars dirtied by the enslavers' faces from behind the purse lining. Even now, I am wealthy in old wisdoms and forgotten stories. So prosperous am I in memory and muse. Until I can pay the rent in moon blood and poetry, may my knowing ancestors remind me that my worth is unbound to small numbers on a bright screen or round trinkets in a pouch. My currencies are called *beauty*, *freedom*, *vitality*, and *art*, and tonight, when the money is gone, I bid the hidden intelligence of the universe keep my kin and me fed, safe, warm, and well, resourcing me in giving and receiving these, my truest treasures.

### 1.11. The Insomniac's Song
*Lament of the Sleepless Witch*

Sometimes there is much to be learned during the sleepless hours, much to be witnessed in the shadows of our rooms when our eyes refuse to close. The visionary's sleep is disturbed by countless considerations, errant thoughts, and the residual slop of waking hours. When the sleepless times come, this is the visionary's prayer.

May I become a living song of wonder this sleepless night. May I become that sleepless Witch who walks with one foot in the dreamlands.

Here, I weave with lids half-closed, humming and braiding the triple threads of hope, grief, and awe around the wild bundles of my memories, calling on that elusive spirit of sleep to come, to wrap its warm and fat-fleshed arms around me and carry me home. When that old ghost finds me at long last, I'll wake inside a dream within a dream, leaving those gifts I crafted on the edge of sleep tucked away in a seer's cave for my wiser ghosts to find.

### 1.12. What We Dare Not Speak
*In Praise of Unpopular Ideas*

No truly revolutionary idea was ever born popular. The visionary is full of sharp opinions that would be – and often are – rejected on the small screens of social media. Sometimes what we dare not speak can orient us toward our work in the world, what our art might illuminate if given a chance to shine. That one word we hold so deeply true that would be rejected so quickly by the masses may be just the one we are here to howl. This prayer is for those secret understandings spoken only on the edges, where the trickster dwells.

Tonight and every night, the world is made by those who dance on the fringes, who have been locked out of the nobleman's house and sent to the woods. There, in the hidden camps where the fox-women tell stories to the wild children, where the old one lights the road with a flame-eyed skull, our tongues can speak the truth. Just maybe, a part of us understands a good secret wants the dark. A revolutionary idea requires rejection, and just maybe, it is the freaks who startle the world into being. To my most unpopular opinions, I raise a glass to the east, wink, and wait for dawn to come.

### 1.13. The Splendor of These Wicked Times
*A Song for Dark Days*

Even now, there is a splendor afoot. Even when the days are wicked, I am met by the *spiritus mundi*. That wild ghost finds me in the most unforeseen places: while weeping for tragedies in faraway places, stacking stones in the woodland for my beloved dead, or befriending a stranger. There, when I least expect her, that holy ghost kisses me on the cheek and reminds me to keep an irrational joy alive in my heart. She sings me a quiet song for dark days and whispers, *Birth always follows disintegration.* She reminds me of life's brevity, smooths my hair, and goes on her way, leaving me with wet eyes and a soft smile. To this older-than-ancient spirit, I say thank you. Thank you for reminding me to tend to these times like I would an ailing child — with great care and an elder's wisdom, with heathen eyes that can see for one hundred million years.

# *2*

# THE BOOK OF WILD LOVERS

*Prayers for Lust, Seduction,*
*and Majestic Relatedness*

*The world wants to lick us alive.* Our cells can sense the seduction in a sunset, in that lustful come-hither song written by the night for every creature on this majestic moss-and-loam-skinned rock we call Earth. There is a part of us who sees the splendor in all things, who understands the beauty of decay and the sensuality of a looming storm. This vital part of us, our inner lover, is the one who stands in awe of these times.

Rarely does the lover find meaning in isolation. They learn through small intimacies between themselves and the beyond-human world. They are wed to the wild, and their prayers are love stories full of longing and eco-lust.

We feed our inner lover by being present to both joy and grief, both quiet dawn and vicious evening wind. If we allow them to step forward from time to time, we learn the power of belonging to the greatest love story ever written. Our inner lover stands behind our inner narrator, the one who distills our vision into a neat plotline we can follow, and waits for the silence, for the open spaces between words of certainty where the savory juice of romance can drip through.

The prayers in The Book of Wild Lovers are love letters to the Holy

Wild. Imagine them being whispered by a shape-shifting vixen who sits in the hollow between two intertwined oaks. She tends this lovers' altar by healing her own heart, by speaking spontaneous poetry channeled up from the roots of these older-than-ancient trees. These are her prayers and yours.

## 2.1. Honeymoon under a Honeyed Moon
*When Lust Finds Us Lonely*

This wicked midnight is going to have its way with me, and I've opened the curtains so that silver-lipped sorceress called moon might bear witness to my rapture. May a lust-drunk memory find me now and lick me alive. May a fallen angel meet me 'neath these sheets and speak Witch to me. A bride to the sweet and holy forbidden, I am, and this is my honeymoon under a honeyed moon.

## 2.2. Winter's Love Song
*When We Are Seduced by the Wilds*

The inner lover's eyes are so keenly attuned, they see beauty in the dark. The lover does not wait for the sun to drip its golden honey on the muck; they see beauty right there in the mud-and-ice fallows. When we sense we are being seduced by even the barren wilds, this is our lover's prayer.

Deep in the mud-and-frost fallows of a late-winter forest, may we hear the troubled love song winter writes for spring. May this heathen hymn sing us alive, these quiet and aching hours when every branch is bare. Here, the chilled verses sting us awake, and the snowscape chorus lures our joylessness into winter's wild dreaming time. These are hallowed evenings, we know. These are frozen dusks haunted by wildflower ghosts, as spring comes creeping. May we listen well to the footfalls of the quickening spirits, letting these small ceremonies of liminal grace have their way with us, one frost-and-honey moonrise at a time.

## 2.3. Prayers of Persephone
*For Cusp-of-Spring Midnights*

The dark feminine dwells inside the mythic temples of underworld Goddesses. They are shadow walkers who have been to hell, and their stories bite us alive, inviting us not only to consider the cyclical nature of our own soulful descents and risings but to find a wicked splendor there in our most initiatory tales.

Some say the gods left these lands long ago, but I say the land is god. I, Persephone, say we are still here. Moan with me.

> *I am the Underworld Queen howling her soul home*
> *I am ruby pomegranate seed and blue-salt seafoam*
> *I am rebirth and death*
> *I am all that is left*
> *I am Persephone*
> *The first and last breath*

Moan with me.

So, here we are again. Here we are again, ready to die and ready to live. Here we are, caught between a life so achingly possible, so ripe with joy, we taste the spice-and-honey hedonism on our tongues and the other, a fallow life so fleshless and cold we call the boneyard our home. Here we are.

So what shall we do?

Moan.

Moan with me. Let me hear that throaty rattle only those mistresses of the underworld make. It sounds like half drowning in pomegranate juice and refusing to die. It sounds like the bones of the undead groaning in the earth below a laughing child's feet. It sounds like that knowing crone who sits atop your ribs and skips stones in your blood, cackling at her own dirty joke, and it sounds like mayhem meeting choice, a storied past meeting an apocalyptic future.

So, go on. Moan with me.

It's the best part of the underground language, you know. That moan means nothing and everything at once, and only those who have sat shaking draped in red satin with a bare back leaning against some wild tree know what I mean. Only those who sat there with a poison apple between their teeth, only those who clawed their way up through the muck of a grave built just for you by someone else's hand can really hear this sound.

Moan with me, and I'll hear you.

Some say the gods left these lands long ago, but I say the land is god. I, Persephone, say we are still here. Moan with me.

Only those with a honey tongue sitting heavy inside a foul mouth, only those who can map the depths of the shadow caves can feel the haunted memories inside that holy sound.

Moan with me. I hear you. Moan with me. I am you.

Some say the gods left these lands long ago, but I say the land is god. I, Persephone, say we are still here. Moan with me, and I'll sing my story for you.

Once in a land so luscious time could not exist, I found myself brimming with an innocence only the old hags remembered. Before this, I remember nothing. I was born fully grown, with a curious hunger for awe and wonder lodged behind my ribs. I was born with a pomegranate-shaped heart woven from ivy and grapevines, and I was born with silver sigils stitched into my skin by moonlight, sewn there by the hooded healer woman who knew my fate before I did, before my name was pitied, before my mother mourned me, and before I was marked in mayhem by my demon lover.

In the days of my innocence, my woven heart pulsed in a rhythm so slow cities would rise and fall in the space between my heartbeats. I was the spirit of the land, and the land was the spirit of me. I was every olive tree and creek bed. I was the smallest river stone and the greatest mountain. I was the mud and the sea. I was the hour before dawn and those long haunted moments before dusk. In the days of my innocence, I was aboveground, and I knew nothing of the shadowlands below.

The world seduced me over and over and over again. Each day was a life lived well, and each night was a small but beauteous death. I lived in rhythm with all things, and all things lived in rhythm with me.

I don't know how it happened. Some say I was hunted. Some say there was a bad bargain, but one day my woven heart began to beat faster and faster. I started to feel the weight of that thing called time, and the days grew colder and colder still. My hair grew brittle, and my silver-stitched skin started to sag and crease. My heart beat faster, and I tasted dirt on my tongue. My heart drummed faster still, and my body hollowed out like a dying tree. I began to age, but I began to hear the songs of the land like I never could before. My beauty was falling all around me like dead leaves, but I was becoming something great. I was breaking out of my smaller skin. I was being reborn, and I could feel my innocence grow hungry for wisdom. I was becoming deep time, and I am her still.

I am the untouched withering wilderness embodied in the paper-soft skin of a woman. I am the fallen fruit and the abandoned hive. I am the shelter forsaken for sweeter ground, and I am the promise of spring turned to the heat of summer turned to the grief of autumn turned to still winter. I am deep time.

Some say the gods left these lands long ago, but I say the land is god. I, Persephone, say we are still here. Moan for me.

I fell into a state my mother didn't understand. I became a dream within a dream. I was here, and I was not here. I was the secret kept by the most melancholic angels — that all the joys and pains of this world are lived out through us, through the creatures who live and die here. We are every story ever written, every comedy and tragedy, every wanderer's fever dream and every seer's stunning vision.

The snows began falling, and I took to the underworld with a lover who promised me much, who vowed to hear my strange songs and see my face even when the last of my flesh had fallen from my bones. My mother didn't understand, and she didn't need to.

Fools say I was broken by him. Fools say I was stolen and caged and kept against my will. Fools say I was a poor girl lost to an old magick I couldn't understand. They pitied me, those fools, but the knowing ones grant me the great story I deserve. The underworld was my choice. My dark lover was handpicked by me, and I suffered in the name of no one but that beast called linearity.

Part of me is still there with him, curled against his gnarled body, him curing me and me curing him. Part of me is still a bride to my first devil, and part of me is still letting the firelight have its way with me, letting his long fingers trace the secret sigils on my skin. Part of me is perpetually living a midwinter, and part of my woven-from-ivy heart broke off and stayed there seeding the subterranean forest. Part of me remains there, just as part of you remains in every memory that marked you well.

Don't run from it. There's no point. Those old stories are in there anyway. Let them loose. Let them loose and moan with me.

Some say the gods left these lands long ago, but I say the land is god. I, Persephone, say we are still here. Moan with me.

I am the cold winter hell you remember, and I am the wildflowers in bloom. I am paradox. I am fallen angel and the risen demon. I am the underworld Goddess returned with pomegranate juice running down her chin and wicked poetry dripping from her lips. You know me. I see you. You know me. I am you.

Some say the gods left these lands long ago, but I say the land is god. I, Persephone, say we are still here. Moan with me.

I am forbidden fruit eaten at just the right time. I am ascended with dirt under my nails and the memory of the wickedest monsters breeding and feeding. I am the shadow and the light, the eternal winter storm and the never-ending spring sun-shower. I am where memory meets this moment, and I am every Witch who's ever been to the underground.

So, here we come. Here we come with the stories no one shares. Here we come with grief songs in our ivy-woven hearts and serpentine love poetry snaking 'round our inner thighs.

Some say the gods left these lands long ago, but I say the land is god. I, Persephone, say we are still here. Moan with me.

*I am the Underworld Queen howling her soul home*
*I am ruby pomegranate seed and blue-salt seafoam*
*I am rebirth and death*
*I am all that is left*
*I am Persephone*
*The first and last breath*

## 2.4. Wildflower Honey and Horned Shadows
*When a Darker Muse Calls*

When the warmer winds blow hard, these dreams of mine are haunted by a long-horned shadow. Wildflower-honey poetry drips from their tongue, and their veins run red with wine, this wanton and wonderful beast. Their bark-and-stone skin is kissed by moss and stubborn frost, and I call them my hallowed lover, my fairy-tale devil, my muse. To you, my most splendid monster, I say welcome. Have your wicked way with me before the summer sun swallows us both whole.

## 2.5. Under the Same Stars
*A Soft Bandage for an Old Cut*

The inner lover finds a seed of meaning in all relationships, even those whose stories have come to an end. When the ghosts of old lovers haunt, this is a prayer that stirs the heart.

You and I dream under the same stars, my wounded love. Though we live better apart, I still keep a room open for the ghost of your memory; you'll find the door ajar should you wish to visit the haunted house of my heart, should you dare to think of me, too. I'll put the kettle on.

## 2.6. Alone, and So
*A Healing Song for Leaving a Lover*

Long hours have I lived in love with our shared story. Every morning was a once-upon-a-time, and I was full of faith in our happily-ever-after. Now the only certainty I have packed in my bag is this: I must go. I must go alone, and so tonight I pray to my soul protectors who have seen such things before. I invite my whole and well ones to come near me when I close the door on our dying bond, when I leave one last love letter on the doorstep that reads: *This is my healing song for the severance and my vow to leave you well. May we each be far more blessed by life's beauty apart than we were together, and may we remember the moments when our story was good.* And so it is.

## 2.7. A Holy Parting of Hands
### *To Speak while the Ink Dries on Divorce Papers*

Signing a contract is a small ceremony, for better or worse. Sometimes a divorce demands more celebration than a wedding, and sometimes the inner lover needs a ritual nourishment when hands part; if so, this is the lover's prayer.

I wish you well, as our hands part forever. Let's bury our rings in a sacred grove, our last shared ritual. There, let's break bread at sunset and remember that one wild song that set our hope soaring so long ago. We'll sing the first verse together, the chorus while we walk away, and the song's end we'll hum alone as we head separately into our solitary midnights. There, we wait for the sure-to-come dawn, certain our story was scripted for a reason.

## 2.8. Twin Hearts for a Time
### *To Nourish a New Kinship*

The slow dance of gratitude and grief is burning away what remains of the shredded veil between the seen and the unseen. Something wild brought us together, you know. I tasted fate on my tongue when I saw you. Now you and I are twin hearts for a time, made so by shared laughter and happenstance. I promise to keep my more vicious demons at bay and call you friend, as we stand on the narrow edge between possibility and impossibility. I vow to nourish this kinship with conversation, deep listening, and gifts of bread, poetry, and prairie sage.

## 2.9. Your Sister-in-Lawlessness
### *To Awaken the Inner Heat*

The dusk is full of madness tonight, and I'm opening my legs to the moon. I've spent those last mournful days of winter weaving lingerie from lichen, mist, and longing. I've built a forest bed from wolf fur, heron feathers, and melting snow, and I'm naming this my solitary ritual of homecoming, of tending the fires of extreme desire. To my sullen self I say, *Come with me.* To my inner weeping one I say, *Follow me, your cunning sister-in-lawlessness.* These are the wildest days, after all, and I'm seducing my better self into being one bare-breasted ceremony at a time.

### 2.10. Find Me
*For a Lover Not Yet Found*

When you wake with a strange, fresh heat on your neck, remember the shape of my breath from your wickedest dream. *Find me,* I whispered. Find me in a forest full of wolf-kings, owl-women, and forgotten fairy tales. Find me curled inside the hollowed corpse of a long-limbed oak. Find me and speak of old gods and their shape-shifting mistresses. Bring me an offering of wildflowers and blood, and I'll gift you a glimpse of my rose-petal tongue in return. Kneel and build an altar at my feet from snakeskin and sunstones, singing of how summer seduces spring into being in a language only we know, and I vow to make you a memory so mighty it sets time and space to shake.

### 2.11. Memoir of the Oak Lover's Dedicant
*To Invoke the Bliss of a Spring Well Lived*

The silver tongue of that thinning moon was licking me in just the right places, and I crept from my bed like a lust-drunk and lonely wolf leaving the solace of her too-familiar and colorless den. My favor was for the wild and strange, you see. My hackles were raised in the name of beastly pleasure and creaturely delight. The Beltane fever was upon me, and I remembered what it meant to crawl close to the earth, to seduce the pale green blades to rise and penetrate the soft wet of ground, destined to wail with ecstasy when the first beam of dawn strikes them. I remembered the blush of the stretching petals and the virility of the thorns.

Can you hear them, those hungry unfurling ferns and hot-pink aching buds? Theirs is such primal poetry, such hedonistic hymns. This is the night of the midspring huntress, and I've set my ear to those slow-thrusting songs of breath and body, of groaning branch and thirsty root.

Just at the witching hour, I'll press the bones of my bare back hard into bark and fall into that mad sort of short-lived love with a knotty, naughty oak. She'll heave with the wanting of my exhale, and I'll hiss long and deep into her shameless veins. On and on it will go. I'll breathe and get breathed, slow like the lapping of the calmest waves on forgiving sand, then so fiercely with all the surging erotic fury of a summer storm.

Just before that arrogant sun rises, all will go lightning bright, and that boiling blood of mine will turn to lava. My ancient lover will swallow me whole, and I'll become the holy howling pulse of heathen memory.

Here, I am bride to the forbidden, and my feeling flesh is a Pagan altar to the oldest devotion, to that long-forgotten love between the human animal and these green, gruff gods. Here, I am wordless prayer. I am whole-soul reverence, and I belong to these wilds. I am a living wide-hipped, wet-lipped incantation. I am a breast-to-bark sculpture with a slow-searching and adventurous tongue. I am unsweetened, raw, sharp-clawed demand, then I am the billowed and precious sugar of surrender. I dream. I am dreamt. I dream. I am dreamt. I die into a dark and dancing sea of perpetual primordial yearning, and all is alive within me. I am alive in all.

I am a sweat-beaded skin-drum thundering a ceaseless song. I am a willing offering to these hallowed grounds, to my beloved dead, and to her, my ancient enchantress, my twig-handed lord. I'll sleep satiated on her moss, my ribs caressed toward a dreamscape at long last by her thin-limbed shadows, and I'll wake just in time to see the evening bale fires burn.

## 2.12. Initiation by Axe
### *A Bedtime Story for Handless Maidens and Wild Kings*

Some stories have many names. "The Handless Maiden" is a story of Germanic origin, an initiatory story of wounding and healing, ancestral protection and finding the wholeness of the soul. Also known as "The Girl with Silver Hands" and "The Maiden without Hands," this story houses many archetypes and their lessons. Here, we find the trickster as devil, the ruler and lover as king, the caregiver as gardener, the newborn babe as innocent, and the royal magician as mage. We find a maiden who is bound by her father's bad bargain, and we trace her initiation journey from the dark forest to the house of the wild ones.

This story finds a home in The Book of Wild Lovers not because it is solely a love story but because of the archetypal relationships we uncover along the handless maiden's journey. The lover archetype gathers meaning from relating to others, and along the maiden's journey, we find many encounters between the archetypes that illuminate parts of our own story, the personal plot twists in our own tales of initiation where we were set on another path entirely, not because we met the right person at the right time or the wrong person at the wrong time but because we somehow stayed a step ahead, listening keenly to the future self who calls us forward.

Our initiations — our experiences of death, liminality, and rebirth — do not occur in a vacuum. While there are parts of all three stages when solitude is necessary, relationships tend to play an integral role in these life chapters when the deepest transformation occurs. Notice which parts of the handless maiden's journey mirror your own, and notice who the archetypes represent in your story. Of course, as always, consider how all characters are, have been, or could be an inner part of you and what wisdom can be gleaned from their encounters with one another. Lastly and most importantly, name the questions you have that linger after the story ends. Sometimes, as in dreams, the questions that remain after a story's apparent resolution are the questions of your life.

*The lovers' drums of autumn come*
*Thrum, thrum, thrum*

Once in a time long gone that strangely still is, an ordinary family lived in extraordinary times. The patriarch was a proud man in the humblest of professions. A miller by trade, he was. The matriarch was a healer who had forgotten herself, and the two of them had a lone daughter who, try as she might, could not escape the plight she was born to.

One autumn evening when the winds were shifting and the moon was waxing, the miller went into the wild woodland to gather kindling to cook what was to be a very meager supper. The twisted trees were witness to his despair, and the nightbirds sounded a mourning song for the miller's brighter days. He was a man alone and shrouded in self-pity at sundown, and this was a dangerous situation. Every twig he gathered pierced his pride like a pin, and by moonrise, he was leaning against a wild oak and lamenting the whole of his life. He wept and bemoaned every choice that led him here to this wretched moment, and in this tender and wounded underground, a shadow man found him.

"What's brought you to this state, man?" the shadow asked, poking the miller's cheek with a long-nailed finger that seared the sobbing man's flesh. Marked he was, in that moment, but his eyes were so blurred with tears that he could barely see the dark figure before him.

"Oh, why —" the miller started to answer, but the shadow interrupted him.

"It's none of my business, of course, but perhaps I might offer you some help."

The miller began blinking away the tears, and he started to see the otherworldly nature of this shadow. Wild horns and cloven hooves, this creature had, and a long, forked tail, too.

"How would you like it, my dear miller, if you could enjoy riches beyond your wildest dreams? What if your wife could wear the finest dresses? What if you never had to work another day in your life, and yet your table could be brimming with the sweetest cakes and smoothest whiskey?"

In that moment, the miller knew this shadow to be the devil himself, but do remember, the man was in dire straits. He had all but given up on life itself, you see, and being so close to death, so in your depths, invites a certain kinship with these devils.

It's so easy to judge, I know, but consider your darkest moment. If a devil had shown himself in that moment and offered to drag you from your depths and gift you with all you desire, you might have taken that bargain, and you know it.

"Drop those twigs. You won't need them, after all. Why, all you need to do is say the word and you'll return home to the grandest castle you've ever seen. A house full of servants, a bountiful table, and let's not forget the gold."

"The gold?" asked the miller.

"Oh yes. You, my dear miller, shall be the richest man for miles and miles in every direction. What do you say to that?"

The miller swallowed. "I'd say, what's the catch?"

"No catch. Why, in exchange for all that I've offered, I only want what stands behind your house. That's all. Nothing more. Nothing less."

The miller thought for a moment. "Well, all that stands behind my house is an old apple tree, so ..."

The miller paused, and it seemed great empires rose and fell in that decisive moment. There would be before this and after this, and the miller would never be able to undo his words.

"You have a deal."

The devil smiled.

"All the riches I could ever want in exchange for what stands behind my house. Yes. Yes, surely you have a deal."

The miller had that complicated feeling after he finished his sentence, that nagging sense that he should try to take it back, that it was just too good to be true, but the promise of having all his fears eased was consuming all the space in his aching heart now.

"Wonderful!" The devil leaped high in the air and curled his tail around a low branch. "I'll return in three years' time to collect what's due. In the meantime, do enjoy your new extravagant lifestyle, miller. People might call you many things, but 'poor' will not be one of them."

And with those words, the devil was gone.

The miller ran for home, suddenly dressed in finer clothes than he'd ever worn. By now, the Ancestors' Moon was high and full in the sky, and he could hear his wife squealing with — what? Joy? He had not heard this sound in a very, very long time.

"Husband! Husband!" his wife called over the heath, and he could see the turrets rising high in the air where his house used to stand. A massive castle stood in the place of his falling-down hut, and his wife was wearing what appeared to be a majestic silk gown.

"What has happened? What strange blessings are these?" The miller's wife appeared more concerned than happy, and rightfully so.

The miller told her everything, about his moment of self-pity and the shadow who saved him, and his wife named the creature for what he was.

"You know better, husband! What did you promise him in return for this superficial finery?"

The miller smiled, pleased with himself. "Woman, that's the best part! All I offered in exchange was our apple tree!"

The wife frowned.

"Now, I know you love that tree, but surely with this wealth we can plant a whole orchard! We can plant a hundred orchards!"

"Husband, I know you're no fool, but do tell me exactly what the devil asked for in return for this luxury."

The miller thought for a moment, recalling what he still believed was the luckiest moment of his life, and then he said, "He only asked for what stood behind the house, and there's only that old apple tree there."

The wife clutched her heart, shocked.

"Woman, it barely gives any fruit anymore. It's half-dead. I don't understand —"

The wife began weeping now.

"I'll give you all the apple trees in the world, my love!" The miller tried to soothe her, but she was in quite the state, and it was more than an hour before she had calmed enough to say the words that would nearly stop the miller's heart.

"Husband, the apple tree stands behind the house, yes, but our daughter has been behind the house all evening. You have traded our daughter to the devil."

*The lovers' drums of autumn come*
*Thrum, thrum, thrum*

They spent the night weeping now, the miller and his wife, and the mourning doves woke near them at dawn to remind them of their terrible plight. In time, though, they half forgot the fate that was to befall them. The miller and his wife spent their next years in a state of masked melancholy, unable to enjoy their wealth and fearful for their daughter, who was as yet unmarked by the pain of the world, but they convinced themselves in time that perhaps the entire deal with the devil had been imagined. Three years is a long while, and they chose complete denial over any strategy, over any forethought that might save their daughter. When the three-year anniversary of the terrible bargain approached, the miller and his wife had no plan.

"We need to tell her what's to happen," the miller's wife said one morning, watching her daughter gathering nettles. "The third anniversary of your bargain is looming, and she needs to prepare herself."

The miller held his head in his hands and said nothing.

"We'll tell her tonight," the miller's wife affirmed, and that night, beneath July's Blessing Moon, the small family sat before a bountiful table. They ate mostly in silence, but the daughter began softly weeping at the meal's end.

"Why do you weep, my girl?" asked the mother, hopeful that the maiden had somehow realized her fate on her own, sparing them the horrific duty of telling her the devil was about to take her away forever.

"I'm just so incredibly grateful," the daughter said through her sobbing. "Why, it was only three years ago that we were so poor. We scarcely had wood for our fire and now, look! Look at this meal before us, and the fine clothes we wear! What a gift my father is to us. He has provided so well." The daughter continued her teary speech, and her words overwhelmed the miller, weighing his shoulders down with that heavy shroud called guilt. He stood and left the table wordlessly, and later that evening, he watched from the window while his wife met his daughter gathering nettles near the apple tree.

He watched and wept while his wife spoke lovingly to the daughter he had unwittingly betrayed, though he could not hear the words that were exchanged. He saw his daughter's shocked expression, and he watched the basket of nettles drop from her shaking hands. He wept, and he watched. He wept and watched while the women who were his whole world held one another until dusk fell, and he wept and watched his wife smooth his daughter's hair and rock her in her arms as if she were again a babe with a scraped knee.

For months, the miller was too ashamed to speak to his daughter, but she spent much of that time locked alone in her room, saying only a few words to her mother and going weeks without eating.

*The lovers' drums of autumn come*
*Thrum, thrum, thrum*

With the full Ancestors' Moon came the fateful night. The maiden walked from her room wearing a white tunic she had stitched with her own hands. She said nothing to her parents, walking straight out of the house, past the apple tree, and into the dark forest.

There, she bathed in the stream near their home at moonrise, and the water knew her skin. She washed away her shame in that solitary ceremony of reclamation. She washed away her guilt over choices not made, her rage against her fool of a father, her resentment against her bitter place in the world, and every dark regret she'd accumulated in her short life.

To the water, she said thank you.

She washed away the unspoken words, the wounds of young womanhood, and the unnamable sorrows.

To the water, she said thank you.

She began bleeding from that deep well of mystery between her legs then, and her magick mingled with the holiness of the sacred waters. She washed away the hardness in her heart and the softness in her voice.

To the water, she said thank you.

She could feel the shadow coming for her, and she whispered a prayer of protection to the north:

"To the mountain women of my bloodline, to the winter wolves and the bone-witches, come to me and protect my body on this night."

To the water, to the north, she said thank you.

She cupped her hand between her legs and let the blood pool in her palm, and she whispered to the east.

"To the hawks, the eagles, and the ravens, to the wild dawn and the flame-tending Priestesses, come to me and protect me on this night."

To the water, to her blood, to the east, she said thank you.

She painted a once-and-future symbol on her forehead in red, and to the south, she whispered: "To the fire dancers and the salamanders, to the serpentine queens, protect me on this, the night of all nights."

To the water, to her blood, to the ancestors, to the south, she said thank you.

Lastly, she stood in the shallows, naked as she'd been born to this world, and she raised her arms high to the west.

"To the ghosts of the grandmothers who walk with me, to the great mystery and the hallowed waters, wells, and seas, protect me on this night when the devil is coming for your daughter."

To the water, to her blood, to the ancestors, to the ghosts, to the west, she said thank you.

Cleansed by her own initiatory ritual, she walked home while the blood flowed down her legs to the ground. The miller and his wife watched with horror while their daughter emerged from the woods with a scarlet-stained dress and star on her forehead.

Her mother could see the spectral figures walking with her, but the miller could see only his daughter's blood, and he was terrified.

The daughter began walking in slow clockwise circles around the apple tree now, creating a red ring of blood on the ground with every footfall, and then she stood with her back to the bark.

The devil appeared from the shadows just when the wind stopped and the clouds parted, and the miller and his wife began begging him to leave their daughter be. They bade him take back all their fortune, and they promised to not meddle in the Otherworld again.

The devil refused, and the daughter stood silent with eyes closed.

"She is mine," the devil hissed, looking far more menacing than he did that day in the woods. "I'll be claiming her on this night."

He reached for her then, but he could not cross the circle of blood. For hours he tried, getting burned each time he tried to step across her ring of protection.

"Ah! She's too clean!" he wailed finally. "I cannot get her." He grew thirty feet tall in that moment, and he stomped so hard like a petulant child that the ground shook beneath them all. "You," he howled to the miller. "You must keep your daughter from bathing for three moons, and then I shall return to claim what's mine."

The miller started to protest, but the devil silenced him: "If you do not do as I say, all you love will wither and die a painful and slow death. Your flesh will turn to leather; your tongue will rot in your mouth. Your daughter must be dirty when I return for her or your whole world will fall to dust."

The devil vanished then, and the daughter stayed stone-still until dawn, sleeping in her own blood and waking covered in fresh dew and earth. She spoke to no one over those next three moons, and she slept under the apple tree even when autumn turned toward winter, letting her hair become matted with mud, dirt gathering beneath her nails, and her white dress turning to gray stained with red.

The devil came to collect her beneath the Imbolc Moon, and when she saw him, she wept the most righteous tears, tears that ran in rivers down her cheeks and fell onto her arms and hands, washing away the grime that had gathered there and cleansing her skin.

When the devil reached for her hands, he shrieked in horror, for the tears of the maiden burned him. Again and again, he tried to take her hands. Again and again, he failed. The maiden kept weeping, and the tears kept streaming, and the devil kept reaching, and the beast kept screaming.

To her tears, she said thank you.

Finally, the devil gave up and gave his most insidious order yet to the miller: "You must sever your daughter's hands," he growled. "You must cut them from her body. When I return at the equinox, I want to find your daughter handless and unwashed."

The miller was stunned into silence, but his wife protested with passion: "No, devil! The deal is undone. You have tried to claim her twice now and failed. She is not meant for you. Go away from this place and never return!"

The devil seemed marked by the woman's words, but he resigned himself to claiming this maiden as his own: "Woman, if you do not do as I say, you and your daughter will die the most painful deaths you can imagine. You will forget your names, and all you love will suffer so greatly, they'll tell stories of your anguish for thousands of years."

With those words, he was gone.

The unwashed daughter spent the next moons singing prayers and speaking to no one. She'd gone mad, her parents thought. Every night, though the snows fell, she slept under the apple tree with a humble fire to keep her heart beating. The miller and his wife brought her food but left her be until the evening before the equinox.

The miller had been too ashamed to speak to his daughter at all for many months, but he approached her slowly now.

She was slouched on the ground in an unnatural shape, her head lulled to the side and the firelight flickering on her dirt-caked face. She was humming lightly to herself and watching the flames with great intent, lips blue with cold, smoke washing away her rational and reasonable mind.

To the smoke, she said thank you.

The miller did not recognize her, this wretched creature, and he felt strangely unworthy.

"Daughter," he started. "Daughter, I will do whatever you wish. We could try to run. We could try to reason with him."

The maiden started laughing then, gently at first and then a mad laughter that sent the miller's spine quivering.

Her laughter turned to weeping then, and this went on for quite some time while the miller stood helplessly at the fireside wondering if his daughter had forgotten how to speak, wondering what her mind had become.

To her madness, she said thank you.

Long past midnight, she fell into silence, and the miller stoked the fire hotter and moved to wrap her in a blanket.

"Father," she whispered with eyes closed. "You were supposed to protect me from such things." Her words were faint, and she slipped into a sleep while the miller wept.

They woke huddled together with the fire a pile of smoking coals and the miller's wife screaming.

The devil was taunting her, and the miller ran to the mother of his child.

"Devil! Leave her be!" But the devil kept leaping and dancing and scorching the woman's skin. Such was the commotion that no one noticed the daughter going into the barn and returning with the silver axe, but they saw her now.

The maiden stood in that rare state of depth that only the spirits know, a state of purposed grace. The snow fell into her knotted hair, and her face had lost all expression.

"Do what you must, Father," she said. "This was your bargain, after all."

She handed him the axe while the devil and the mother stood still.

"I — I can't," said the miller. "I can't do it."

The devil opened his mouth to make his usual threats, but the maiden raised her hand to silence him.

"You can. You made the deal. You finish it." She knelt and put her wrists on the chopping block. "Do it!"

All manner of apology poured from his lips while he raised the axe high in the air and landed it with a swift clang, severing both her hands at once.

She wailed in the greatest agony she'd ever known, and then she kept weeping. Her tears flowed down her arms and salted and cleansed her wounds, and when the devil reached for her with a great smile on his face, he found he could not claim her, for her tears had again washed away the muck.

To her tears, she said thank you.

Without a word, knowing he could never return, knowing his third failure broke the bargain forever, the devil vanished and with him all their great fortune.

The miller and his wife were suddenly in rags. Their immense estate had shrunk to the shack it once was, and their handless maiden stood and stripped herself of her once-white dress. She used her teeth and her toes to wrap her stumps in the fabric, and then without a word to her parents, she buried her face deep into the cooling ashes of the fire and set off naked into the woods while the winds of March howled.

To the ashes of her life, she said thank you.

*The lovers' drums of springtime come*
*Thrum, thrum, thrum*

The handless maiden wandered in her own underworld for many, many moons. Spring came and went, as did the summer. Some said they could hear her wailing like a banshee when the autumn moons were new, and she found herself again at midwinter alone with her story.

To her solitude, to her story, she said thank you.

She forgot the names given her, and she forgot where she'd come from.

To her namelessness, she said thank you.

She ate of the earth, of the berries and the fungi, and she drank of the same stream that had cleansed her all those years ago.

To the land, she said thank you.

In her strange state, she was close to the Otherworld, and she was well protected.

To the Otherworld, she said thank you.

When her wandering had stripped away all she was, only then did she happen upon a grand garden surrounded by a wide and swift-running moat. In the garden stood immense pear trees with the ripest of fruit, and the handless maiden hungered for sweetness for the first time in a long, long while.

She didn't know it, but the king's gardener was watching when the handless maiden was suddenly shadowed by a mist-white figure that waved its hand and the moat dried up. He watched while the strange naked creature crossed the moat into the garden, and he watched while the mist spirit bent the pear branch down so the maiden might eat. He watched, stunned still, as she ate a single pear right off the branch and then returned to the shadows of the forest while the moat swelled to fullness again.

The next day, the king came to the garden to count his fruit like he often did, and he noticed a single pear was missing.

"Gardener, someone has robbed me of one of my finest pears! Do you know how this came to be?"

The gardener was still near speechless from what he'd witnessed the night before, but he told the king all he'd seen.

The king knew his gardener to be trustworthy, and though the story seemed more fantasy than truth, he believed his land keeper. That night, he called the magician to stand watch with them and wait for the handless maiden and the mist spirit, and, sure enough, right at the witching hour, the two appeared, the moat dried up, they crossed into the garden, and the pear tree bent so the handless creature could eat.

"What is she?" the king asked the magician. "You have seen such things before, mage. Is she a spirit, or is she human?"

The three watchmen stepped from the shadows now and approached the mist spirit and the maiden.

"I believe…" the magician began, looking into the mysterious eyes of the handless maiden. "I believe she is both."

With his words, the mist spirit disappeared, and the king fell irrevocably in love with the woman.

*The lovers' drums of autumn come*
*Thrum, thrum, thrum*

The handless maiden lived in the castle for a time, and as the new Ancestors' Moon dawned, she accepted a proposal of marriage from the young king. She had great wealth and finery and, for the first time in a long while, a good deal of joy. She was still, however, without her hands. The king's mother grew fond of the handless maiden, and the woman felt as though she had protectors again.

The evening before the wedding, the night before the full Ancestors' Moon, the king knocked on the handless maiden's door and offered her a gift, two intricately designed silver hands nested grandly in an ornately carved wooden box.

"I want to give you all you never had," the king promised, kneeling.

The handless maiden looked at her king and for the first time saw a bit of her father in him.

"But I've had hands before," she corrected. "They were stolen from me, cut from my body with a silver axe made of the same metal as your gift. You would give me hands made from the same material as the weapon that cut them from me."

The king now saw the folly in his gift, and he rose from the floor.

"I do wish to be your wife, dear king," the handless maiden assured him. "But you cannot make my hands grow back."

The king listened, and he understood. The two were married the next day and lived for one full year quite happily, before the trickster came creeping once more.

*The lovers' drums of autumn come*
*Thrum, thrum, thrum*

Very near to their first anniversary, the king was called away to war. The handless queen was heavily pregnant and bade him to stay, but he was unable to refuse the request of his brethren.

"As soon as she gives birth," the king ordered his mother, "send for me. I'll come home at once."

And so the king left his handless queen, and just as the first snow was falling, the handless maiden became mother to a healthy and fat babe. The king's mother sent word to her son just as she was told, but the messenger was met by the same devil that had met the handless queen's father so many years ago. He was lulled into a heavy sleep, and the trickster switched the message to say the queen had given birth to a dog.

The king received the message, wept a great deal, and then sent word for the queen to be well protected during what must be a very difficult time in her life, but, again, the messenger was lulled to sleep and the king's kind message was switched to an order to kill the queen and her babe at once.

The king's mother received the message and refused it. "My son could not possibly have sent this!" she said. "He would never ask such a thing!"

But the king's men believed it to be an order, and they planned to kill the queen and her babe the next morning.

That night, under the Beltane Moon, the king's mother helped the queen wrap the babe to her body and led them into the forest, weeping. She covered the handless mother in a long red veil to protect her from the devils.

To the veil, she said thank you.

The king's mother said, "You must go. You will be protected by these wilds you once knew."

To the wilds, she said thank you.

*The lovers' drums of springtime come*
*Thrum, thrum, thrum*

After the queen was safely off the grounds, the king's mother had a messenger send the king the hearts of a mother deer and her fawn, saying the deed had been done.

When the king received the blood-soaked box and the note, he howled with an anguish that shook the earth and set out to return to his wounded and broken home.

The king, his mother, and the magician all concluded that the devil was to blame for the miscommunication, and the king left his mother in charge of the kingdom while he set out into the forest to find his lost love and his child.

Meanwhile, the queen had traveled farther than she'd ever gone, nursing her babe inside caves and whispering tales of fairies and night creatures to the innocent. The mist spirit followed them, protecting them from the wolves and showing them the way the forward.

To the mist spirit, she said thank you.

On summer solstice, the handless queen happened upon a sanctuary of wild woodland folk. They welcomed the queen and her babe. They taught her the medicines of the forest and the ways of the land spirits. There, in their strange stone temple, the queen came to a new knowing about herself and the world. The women cared for her babe when she was in her depths. They wept with her, and, slowly but surely, over seven years' time, the queen's hands began to grow back, blooming from her wrists anew.

To the house of the wild ones, she said thank you.

The king had been wandering for a long time himself now, and his beard had grown gnarly and knotted. He had twigs in his hair and dirt-caked skin, and he, like the handless maiden on her journey, had forgotten the names given him. Lost in his own dark forest, the lover king moved through his own secret initiations, his own midnight torments and mad moments of ghostly visitation.

To the wilds, he said thank you.

The mist spirit found the king one autumn evening, just as the Ancestors' Moon was nearly full, and led him to the sanctuary of wild men, who gave him food, drink, and song. He asked the wild men if they knew where his woman and child might be, and they told him of the wild women who lived on the mountain. At dawn he searched and searched, remembering the elder wild man's direction that he could find the wild women's sanctuary only when he stopped looking.

To the elders, he said thank you.

Just when the full moon rose, he saw the stone temple, and he saw his queen cradling their child to sleep in her own strong hands. He barely recognized her, for she had become something new. She barely recognized him, for he, too, had become something new. Together, the three of them rode home in the greatest love, whole and well, made so by gratitude and grief.

To love, to the Ancestors' Moon, they said thank you.

*The lovers' drums of autumn come*
*Thrum, thrum, thrum*

## 2.13. To the Mist Spirit
### *A Handless Maiden's Prayer for Ancestral Protection*

Fearful I am, on this dark day when the beasts are howling outside my door. My hands have been severed, lost in a poor bargain made by a fool. I call upon my most protective ancestors now, those way-back-still-here ones who keep watch from the realms of deep time, who whisper words of initiation and gift me sweet dreams though my waking hours are sour. I take sanctuary in the faint shadows of these mist spirits now. I bid them come closer and form a shielding circle around my sacred work, my health, my spirit, and my kin. *Come closer, you heathen warriors and sharp-tongued grannies. Raise your scythes and keep the fires hot. Your wandering daughter needs you now. Come swiftly, as I am forever marked by this moment. Here, I surrender to the remaking of my life, to the restoration of my healer's hands in the house of the wild ones.* And so it is.

# 3

# THE BOOK OF THE BONE-WITCH
## *Prayers for Grievers, Death Walkers,*
## *and Shadow Kin*

**Grief is ever-present in a well-lived life.** Grief reminds us why we were born to this world, orients us toward our greatest purpose, and, if we allow it, tenderizes the hard edges around our heart so gratitude can break through. We can feel joy only as deeply as we feel grief, and our inner bone-witch knows this truth well.

There is a part of us that keeps the tender secrets tucked away, the understandings that might break our spirits into one hundred thousand pieces if we looked too closely. This mystery keeper has no name, but we might call them a death walker. They wear a key around their neck that opens death's door. We fear them, but we are them.

We witness the death-bringer archetype in many forms. In the old stories, the death walker is the wailing banshee, the wild hunt, or the shape-shifting monster who lives in the wilds beyond the wilds, in the places where even the warriors do not dare tread. In the older stories, the death walker is an elemental, a force of nature no more evil or rare than a rough wind.

We all harbor the same knowing as every wild animal; we will someday, in this incarnation, take our last breath. Our body will lie still, and if we are lucky, someone will sing our soul home. The prayers of the death walker are prayers to live well, name change holy, bury the old self, and mark our many initiations in blood.

Imagine these prayers from The Book of the Bone-Witch spoken by a wandering skull-faced crone who walks among the headstones. She leaves gifts on the graves and sings songs in loving memory of lives well lived and the many longings left on deathbeds. These prayers are hers and yours.

### 3.1. Rest in Peace, Wonder, and Pomegranate Seeds
*When the Old Self Dies*

The bone-witch knows small deaths require ritual, too. When the old self dies, when an initiatory chapter in a life story has ended, a small ceremony of death and rebirth is welcome. In these moments, this is the bone-witch's prayer.

Tonight, I take great care in burying a bundle of bones. These are neither the treasured remains of a loved one nor those of a beloved pet gone too soon. Tonight, I bury the bones of who I once was. I'm clawing at the dirt and digging deep with my bare hands, whispering soft spells to my otherworldly witnesses. I'll know the grave is ready when the rain falls, and I'll gently place that bundle in the earth so new life might be born of rot. Grief always wants the ground.

To the one who woke full of regret, I say farewell. To bed with you, you timid creature who tiptoed around fragile men. Here lies the small one who feared the dark. Sleep well in death, you innocent who tried so hard to be good. Rest in peace, wonder, and pomegranate seeds, my old self. I was glad to know you, though your passing brings little sorrow to my reborn heart. I will visit you often in reflection, when I name memory the sharp-tongued mother of my muse, and I shall sing-speak a grief song for your best days.

### 3.2. I Hear You, Reaper
*A Prayer for an Autumn Dusk*

I hear you, reaper. I hear you when you say this wild moon is a platinum chalice forged in the underworld and full of silver honey, mist, and the poetry of Witches lost in the autumn dreaming time. I hear you when you say I should sup from this hallowed cup at dusk, and I hear your haunted song drumming behind my ribs, a feral rhythm echoed by those quiet gods who live inside graveyard trees, who tend the harvest fire, the fire behind all fires on these, the holiest of days. May I learn this song before the long winter comes creeping.

### 3.3. The Hollow-Bellied Hag
*When Colder Winds Blow Hard*

If I were a hollow-bellied hag scrying a death song for this old year from the black-mirror shadows between my ribs, the first line of that song would be hissed with a forked tongue, whisper-spit into the ashes of my youth, and painted with a thick burn salve upon the charred skin of my heart. When the colder winds blow hard, when the nights grow longer and longer still, may I sing this dirge into the boneyard of my memory. I will send it moonward in serpentine spirals of breath that fog in the cold, and I will repent nothing except those bitter hours spent worrying about sagging chins and time's forward march.

### 3.4. My Home That Will Never Be
*A Keening Song for the Unvisited Places*

We mourn for the loss of place, for the homes that will never be. In these moments, the bone-witch sings for our love of land, sea, and sky. Here, this is their prayer.

Never say never, they say, but there is no defeat in honoring fate. There is no failure in tending roots sunk deep in familiar soil, and tonight, I'm bidding the beauty of *here* be the medicine for my pulsing heartache that drums *not there, not there, not there.* May my wail hearken a home-sickness for a life that will not be. May my cry ripple the timelines of my story and, just maybe, may another version of me who lives in that land of wonder hear my keening song, stop, and hum with me, the lost sister. She longs for this place, mayhap, as I long for her home, and together, we will sing for the unvisited places, for the homes that will never be.

### 3.5. This Fallow Ground
*A Song for Our Inner Snow Days*

A heathen soul is wild ground, and we must leave the land fallow for a time, that it be better seeded when warmer winds return. May our winter tears bless the barren snowscapes. May our weary songs be heard by the land spirits, and may the corpse of our despair be buried swiftly and with great care, its grave dug deep under the thick ice of winter's silent wait, its leathery flesh nipped and nibbled away by the ravenous elementals. May our grief seed our gratitude, these early dusks, and may this fallow ground be consecrated now, in all its emptiness. Come spring, may our will bloom lush and green like a woodland forest full of lust. And so it is.

### 3.6. The Parting Soul
*A Heathen Dirge for Miscarriage*

Once, I learned your name in a dream. When I woke, I'd forgotten your face, but your name stays with me, tattooed under my skin by an other-worldly, ancestral scribe. When the full moon shines on my skin many years from now, when the timely moments of wholeness have visited and filled the void you've left with wildflowers, grief songs, and that wily beast called hope, the lunar light will illuminate the silver name of the babe who called my flesh and my dream visions home for a time. To that yet-to-be version of me, I say wait for me; for now, I'm weeping. I'm healing. I'm weeping. I'm healing. To the parting soul, I say find me in my dreams. Never will I forget you or the name emblazoned on my soul's skin.

### 3.7. The Last Gift
*To Whisper When Leaving a Home for the Last Time*

Today, I leave a golden pentagram on the windowsill of this home I have known, loved, decorated, despised, befriended, repaired, and tended these last long years. I draw a secret sigil with moon water on the walls that means gratitude. I sprinkle sea salt where my bed once stood and whisper a prayer for the old lovers, forgotten dreams, and long sleeps that healed my heart here. In this house, I have been wild and tame. I have been hermit and host. Here, I've been the caregiver with an ailing spirit and the vixen full of joy. Today, I remember the miracles that met me at the door, the guests who brought me gifts, and the ghosts who brought me grief. To you, dear house, I thank you, and I leave you one last gift, a memory bundle of the Witch who haunted your halls. Surely no other will live here as I lived. And so it is.

### 3.8. For the Three Fates
*A Spell When the Old Wound Bleeds Again*

Fate is a twisted beast. Some refuse her. Others embrace her in hopes of her befriending their purpose. All are her dedicants. This prayer gives a nod to her existence, a simple homage to the red thread we all follow.

This aching evening finds us warmed by an exquisite cloak woven from thorns, wolf fur, and the bloodstained bandages that once wrapped our old wound, carefully stitched by those three twisted sisters of fate. They invite us to sit by their eternally burning harvest fire, to find a quiet home there while they speak of scars, boneyards, and treasure maps. That wild sister whose head is turned backward brews us a cup of bitter tea from pine smoke and elder wisdom while the hooded one sings us a story of our greatest gifts, of those scripted moments that made us whole. The last sister soaks our cloak with the heavy rains of gratitude and grief, but we wear it well, letting fate's fire dry this soul pelt so it fits like a second skin. And so it is.

### 3.9. Haunted by Hooded Women
*To Remember When Rights Are Stolen*

A Witch who overidentifies with the terror of the Burning Times finds their magick stunted, their spiritual identity caged in a traumatic past where no healing can find them. But there are days when a righteous rage confounds the Witch's soul, when we cannot help but be haunted by hooded healer women who were hunted for their wisdom. On these days, we protest, we petition, we gather, and we pray.

Haunted by hooded women, I am. On these days when the Witchhunters wear black robes, brandish gavels, and hide in their columned palace of stone, I am never alone, for my rage is a hellfire witnessed by my healer ancestors who remember the Burning Times. Here, they bid me cool my molten ire in their crucible that it may become a weapon of words, forged with care and wielded well. Here, they remind me I am the breathing ancestral altar and the living answer to the aching questions howled forth by my forebears as they hid their wisdom under the cover of night, tucking invaluable bundles of the old ways beneath standing stones and oak roots, whispering heathen prayers that their granddaughters be willing to get their hands dirty and dig. I hear their songs now, drowning out the pitiful declarations made by fearful beasts who sit in high places. I hear them, and I sing with them. I hear them, and I remember why I chose to be born here and now, why I chose to name myself Witch.

### 3.10. For You, Dead One
*To Whisper into Graveyard Dirt*

To remember the dead, to write their names inside the holy book of memory that sits open atop our inner altar, is to befriend the wholeness of life. We know a death ritual is not completed in the space of a few hours, and we know our loving ghosts walk with us until we cross the great threshold ourselves. Until then, we remember the dead, and we remember them well.

This season of graveside poetry, disembodied song, and spectral communion, I go to the boneyard. I'm packing only drums, dirges, and the bones of the old self in my bag. I'm singing a song of shadow and mayhem and wandering long into the autumn storm, dancing yet again in my deep soul's cemetery of mythic memory. Here, I remember you, my beloved dead. I remember you for your laughter and outlaw ways. I pour whiskey on the dirt in gratitude for the stories you left on my tongue and the memories you left in my heart. For you, dead one, I am ever thankful.

### 3.11. To You, I Sing
*A Midnight Dirge for a Loved One Gone Too Soon*

So soon did you leave us, our beloved. I opened a window so your soul might fly free. I bid the bright and winged ones carry you on their backs to the world beyond the veil. I'll find you there one day. In the meantime, let me speak of your greatest joys.

### 3.12. The Banshee's Wail
*To Howl into a Haunted Room*

Speaking the language of ghosts means learning the poetry of the wounded or lost ones, those bound to a place by spectral rebellion or obligation, those spirits who never found the otherworldly maps tucked away by their own beloved dead. To them, on this most holy day, I say the door is still open. The last ship sailing to the Isle of the Dead is still in port, and you're holding a one-way ticket. Tell me, ghost: Do you need to stay? Are you still bound here by ties to the living, or do you simply fear the unknown? You are a babe caught in the birth canal. This room is a dry, dusty womb tomb; you don't need to stay. You have grown too big for this heavy world. Go into the silver-diamond light as the infant does, full of faith that a caring face awaits, knowing that your wild soul will not be lost, trusting you may, in time, begin again. And so it is.

### 3.13. By Blood and Bone
*A Prayer for the Dead*

In a society that fears death and locks its elders away, to remember our dead regularly is radical. To tell their stories, be witnessed, and speak their names is a small rebellion against an overculture that wishes us to forget our own mortality. When memories of your most beloved dead come to haunt, this is the bone-witch's prayer.

This hallowed evening when the dead walk heavy on the Earth, may we raise a glass, shed a lone tear for truth, and walk with courage into the night surrounded by the ghosts who know us best. With hearts haunted and heavy, we'll stand on a high hill, face west, and ring a silver bell for every soul in spirit who left their mark upon our stories, who kissed our memories with righteous rebellion and wild joy. To our dead, we say thank you. For you, tonight and every night, we sing.

∽◡✄

# 4

# THE BOOK OF THE HEATHEN QUEEN

*Prayers for Empowerment,*
*Sovereignty, and Truth Telling*

*There are days when our world* is a library full of books written by royals and their so-called holy men, but the greatest stories might be those that have been dismissed as tales for children. In fairy tales, we find the whole of human psychology. What's more, we find where the mind meets the wild, where the doors to initiation are always open. In a fairy tale, every character is you. You are the sick king and the vengeful queen. You are the fool and the seer, the lying fox and the shunned Witch. These stories have much to teach us about our inner sovereignty and our loudmouthed rulers, stubborn queens, and protective lawmakers.

The archetype of the ruler or sovereign is a common one. We all know the faces of the ones who dwell in the castle. We swim in the stories of kings, after all. More rarely do we consider the role of our many inner rulers in shaping our personal myths, the smaller stories of our lives. Sometimes our inner rulers, like the governing laws and norms inherent in the overculture, are so familiar we no longer see them. Their voices speak in dry maxims with that's-just-the-way-it-is authority. These inner royals may have been born before we were born, nested inside our psyche through indoctrination and socialization, or they may have been created out of a need to protect ourselves, to stay safe and keep out of the dark forests where the greatest initiations occur.

At its most whole, the ruler archetype tends the boundaries of our psyche and sits in service to our art, whatever our art may be. They protect our heart without building a thick wall that keeps the teachers who might trouble us into growth locked out, and they guard the vulnerable pieces of our souls and our world fiercely and with unmatched mastery. Severed from heart and art, the ruler becomes ravenous for power, but we all have an inner heathen queen who sits inside the palace of our mind and waits to be consulted. Her concern is for the freedom of self and others, and she requires the offering of our attention if she is to speak. Her prayers are for the wild children, for courage, and for the emboldening of the voices we rarely hear, the stories left out of the kings' books. These prayers are hers and yours.

### 4.1. A Petition to the Unseen Royals
*To Cease the Wavering*

Wild horses are running through my woodland dreamscapes, and I'm inviting a crownless king to visit me on the misty bridge between fantasy and desire. I know what I want, this thirsty midnight. I know what offerings I require to satiate my heathen hunger, and I'm calling my ache home to cook in my most regal cauldron of becoming. Make manifest this dream vision of mine, I say. This is my petition to the unseen royals who hide in the lawless shadows, who secretly make the world and carry no debts to that vicious creditor called morality. Only they can taste the purity of my want, these Pagans before there were Pagans, and only they are permitted room in the spellbound castle of my Witch's mind. Tonight, as a red moon rises, I will cease my wavering and name this want real. Already, it is mine. Already, I feel its weight in my hands. And so it is.

### 4.2. By Raptor's Claw and Wolf's Fang
*A Prayer for Brutal Wisdom*

There are times we grow weary of the sweet maxims and sugar-coated anecdotes meant to please the masses. These are the tell-it-like-it-is times, the chapters in our story that want a forked tongue to hiss hellfire and a one-eyed seer to whisper raw words.

Tonight, I pray for these bitter knowings to be revealed, however harsh they may be. I petition my most resilient forebears come close and slice the skin of my wavering. Here, I wish for the brutal wisdoms cut into the ice by a raptor's claw and the sharp words that live on the end of a wolf's fang. Another day will come when one-size-suits-all advice will not offend me so, but today, by my will, I ask my inner soothsayer for the truth.

### 4.3. Until the Last Golden Fence Falls
*A Prayer for the Heathen Queen's Fire*

Tonight, my inner heathen queen wears a human-leather cloak stitched from the puckered faces of dead kings. Into the fire she tosses the dead wood of power hunger and the dust-and-dirt lint of imperialism. Her kindling was gathered with care in those before-dawn hours when the old world haunts the new world, when ripe possibilities fall from rotten branches. She's welcomed a council of deviants here, this night when the winds are shifting, but for now she sits alone and sings a battle song for the wild children. My prayers are for her to keep this fire burning until those who would kill innocence cough their last breath, until the last golden fence falls and the last Earth killer's fort lies in ruins.

### 4.4. We Dissent
*To Chant in the Wake of Foolish Decisions*

The heathen lives under laws they did not write. The Witch still lives under threat of being bound by systemic ropes tied by the hunters' hands. In these times, we dissent.

Today, the moon has a temper, and that silver-skinned Witch matches my mood. She is marking me with a secret name only I can see, and I'm learning it well, these days of dissent. I'm screaming this name into the old graves, howling it from the hills where gallows once stood to hang women who prayed like I pray, with underworld pomegranate juice dripping from their forked tongues and a ravenous squall behind their eyes. This name is both battle cry and lullaby, both banshee's wail and healer's chant, a silver sigil etched on my heart-skin by that celestial seer called the moon. The moon will not be tethered to injustice, nor will I.

## 4.5. No Ordinary Queen
*To Petition Queen Maeve for a Telling Dream*

Queen Maeve is the Irish Goddess of sovereignty, prosperity, sexuality, and devotion to a land and purpose. She is the wild, sensual, sovereign feminine expressed through indulgence, yes, but she is also a heathen warrior queen who protects the wilds she was born to. This is her prayer.

She's no ordinary queen, you know. That honey-swilling heathen is part wolf, part Priestess, and all wild. She taxes the false prophets and whips the Witch-hunters in the streets. She's made every day a holiday and gifted the land of the nobles to the crows. Bring her a gift of story and ask her for a telling dream. Leave her an offering in the forgotten meadow where the grasses grow long. She's sure to see the worthiness of your want, and should you sleep there amidst the ghosts of her foremothers, you will wake with wine stains on your lips and a haunted drinking song echoing in your mind. I'll find you there.

## 4.6. Breathe Fire
*When Old Words from a Fool Return*

Sometimes the net of an old memory catches our presence, squeezes our heart, and drags us back into an unhealed moment. In these times, we might ask why this sudden spell has been cast upon us. If this memory were an oracle card we pulled in answer to our most pressing question, what would that card mean? In these moments, this is our prayer.

Without warning, old words once spoken by a fool have liquefied my backbone and sent me to the floor. I am a pathetic puddle full of passionless ash. My fire's gone out, and I need the heat of a heathen queen's tongue to lick me alive. I need the spark of red and royal imaginings to startle my sleeping heart awake. Come to me, you flaming-haired Goddess made of muse. Come to me and breathe fire, that I may rise from these hopeless depths. Bite my better soul into being. Name me your bride and carry me over the threshold. And so it is.

### 4.7. The Witch's Antidote
*A Song-Spell for Sucking the Poison Out*

The Fates stuck this thorn in my thumb while I was still in the womb, and I grew around this wound like a well-fed tree. The thorn taught me how to sing, I think, but my voice is my own now, and I'm pulling this old claw from my hand before it's too late. I'm naming hope my healer and holding my heart in tenderness. Tonight, I'm spitting the inherited venom into the flames and calling wisdom my Witch's antidote to the poison of forgetting. And so it is.

### 4.8. The Outlaw Ancestor
*To Bless the Deviants Who Share Our Names*

On this raucous night when the party is sure to go until dawn, I remember you, my outlaw ancestor. I'll leave tobacco and whiskey on the altar and speak well of your crimes, for it's midnights like these when I hear you most clearly, when I love you most dearly. Everything I learned about deviance, I learned from you, and for this I am grateful.

### 4.9. By Oracular Candlelight
*To Open a Family Council Meeting*

A true council allows all voices to be heard. Here, the innocent sits next to the elder. The rebel falls silent while the caregiver speaks, and the heathen queens close their eyes and listen to the quiet sages. Here, all words matter.

We gather tonight to come together in our shared story, listen deep to each voice, and be a living altar. Each of us will light a candle now, a symbol of our unique spark and vital worth. By oracular candlelight, may our most loving and whole ancestors speak through us, reminding us of our kinship, our soul-designed bond, and our common beauty as a family of wisdom keepers. May all voices be heard.

## 4.10. Midnight Memories
### *To Wake a Spontaneous Splendor*

May your midnight memories be joyful, this night. May a spontaneous splendor arise in your dreamscapes and show you a forgotten blessing, a long-lost boon of abundance you once knew but left buried in the brambles of your youth. May this hidden knowing show you the way forward somehow, a bread crumb left on the road in the time of your innocence, a small seed of wisdom tucked away in the wilds of your memory by your inner heathen queen to be found just now, in your haunted dreaming time.

## 4.11. The Silent Sea
### *For the Artist Queen's Mad Moments*

The heathen queen lives with the troubled tension between freedom and stability, wings and roots. Our inner ruler is always writing and rewriting the laws around our work, around what our art really means and how to best fulfill our purpose as a creative human creature without becoming too tethered to our roles and rules. In the moments when this tension feels great, this is our prayer.

When the stillness of the mind cannot come, a soft madness overtakes the soul. We are a hunted fish caught in the vast net of our poetic imaginations, swimming in spirals and crying out for the freedom of quiet, for the dullness of a silent sea we took for granted. Here, we pray for the maker's peace, for the artist's rest, for a dark-moon moment when the next great work has yet to be conceived; and yet, when we visit that silent sea once more, we beg for the net to drop again. The ghost of purpose comes creeping, a shadow on the surface of these untamed waters, and we wonder what freedom really means to a maker who lives to be captured again and again by their own art.

## 4.12. Welcome Home
### *When an Old Wish Comes Back*

The quiet spirit of a forgotten wish is afoot, this strange hour when the oil lamp burns low and the wellspring of ancestral poetry runs dry. I scarcely recognize it, this dream I left orphaned on a doorstep long ago, but here it is again. Here it is, fully grown and on the hunt for its mother, holding that cracked husk that once housed the golden seed of my most fervent desire. To this nameless wish I once called beloved, I say welcome home. Have a seat while I brew you a tea made of earthen nettles, gratitude, and underworld pomegranate juice. Quite welcome here, you are. Tell me of the life you have lived without me, and we'll make travel plans for the sunnier days.

## 4.13. The Thrill of Aliveness
### *For the Evenings That Follow Weary Days*

The inner sovereign requires the thrill of aliveness, a daily dose of vitality that reminds them why they are here. They need their purpose witnessed and their wonder sparked. On the days when these moments do not come, this is the heathen queen's prayer.

A jewel-red rain taps at my window, lit by a stubborn sunset, disturbing my more restful visions and inviting me into the storm. My prayers were for candlelight and the respite of solitude, this night that follows a day swollen with busyness and oozing with ennui, but the god who comes creeping now is called hope. He dares me to dream of a day when the hours move slow as syrup, when I no longer need to remember joy because joy is here, when I've named the thrill of aliveness my long-tongued lover and purpose my most faithful friend. To this wayfaring god who only visits when I least expect him, when I've no room prepared and no welcome song written, I say speak to me. Tell me of that fraying thread called fate and that sharp blade called purpose. Remind me of my soul's worth and heat my tomorrow with holy fire.

∽∾

# 5

# THE BOOK OF THE MOON

*Prayers for Secret Keepers,*
*Midnight Poets, and Fringe Dwellers*

*A trickster's mind is unmatched* in its flexibility, and there are those among us who can hold a million and one possibilities in their hearts at once. The trickster is said to be amoral, their choices neither good nor bad, and it's their unpredictable nature that invites distrust from the masses. When it is considered human to be bound by duality — to feel a compulsion to force all things into neat boxes labeled *this* and *that* — the part of us who skips around our psychic house and tosses these containers to the ground is a wily deviant and grand disrupter.

The trickster's prayers are never for fame or fortune; they are for cloaks of invisibility, necessary shocks to the system, and sweet gifts left at the crossroads. Though never the main character in a story, the trickster is the archetype who invites the plot to unfold, without whom no story could ever exist. From a mythic perspective, many world events and seemingly haphazard forces that expose the cracks in the foundations of our more unjust systems could be called trickster — a disease that shows us how little the overculture cares for the vulnerable, for example, or a drought that brings the possibility of a waterless land to light. Neither the disease nor the drought is *bad*, in and of themselves, nor are they mere symptoms of a greater illness. Though trickster forces will always invite conspiracy theories — a lack of control is uncomfortable, after all — the hand of the trickster always writes the unforeseen plot twists that soften us to new possibilities.

The prayers in The Book of the Moon are spoken with a trickster's tongue. Imagine your inner wily one perched on a low branch of a half-dead tree that grows at the crossroads. They gaze at the moon, beguiled by the oddities of life and singing of shadow men and the golden gifts of fox-women. Their songs are timely ones for a world woven by unseen forces, by the cunning ghosts of our future selves. These prayers are their prayers and yours.

### 5.1. Meeting the Fox on the Road
*A Prayer for Hard Choices*

To trust a fox is a brave endeavor, but I will go the way you say. A hard choice I must make, this night when the owls are calling me toward an unmapped road. Something is tugging at the silver thread wrapped around my heart. Some spirit's hand is curling its finger in my direction, and now here you are, a fox on the road, a vixen with black-mirror eyes. To you, I say: *Show me, trickster. Gift me a treasured vision, a golden symbol that shows me the way. In return, I vow to learn something about your cleverness and see the future in the shadows. In your underground, I will learn all you wish to teach me, fox-woman. Now, lick my wounds and help me make the hard choice.*

### 5.2. Becoming a Star
*For a Poet Who Feels Too Deeply*

In an unprecedented age when artificially intelligent programs dare to write songs, poetry, and stories, we must tend to the artists in their youth. We must tell them to outshine the brightest screen, to brew a medicine only they can. This prayer is for them.

The heat of youth troubles the best poetry into being; it's that electric shock that erupts when hope meets hopelessness, I think. It's that stellar fusion of extreme desire and utter ennui that burns and churns, becoming a star. You, dear poet, are infinite potential embodied in aching skin. You are rough-water rage, rushing sorrow, and lust storm. Let the dam break onto the page and spill its glorious torrent of bile and guile into the world. Hold nothing back. Bid the wildness of language have its way with you over and over again. Let a single word sting you in just the right places. Let a lonely image walk out of the Otherworld and haunt you until you write it alive, and may you remember that the poet is never grander than the poem. May you write the words that want to be written, today and every day.

## 5.3. Offerings on the Mound
### *A Prayer Spoken to the Shadowed One*

Sometimes, when we sense the shadow is afoot, we know an initiatory moment is close. The shadow is who we refuse to be, who we would swear we are not, the fruit of a soulful treasure that fermented and softened into a rot that reeks. When the scent of a shadow edges toward us, nosing its way to the surface of our consciousness, we are close to a creative awakening, one that may just change us forever. These transitions are rarely sweet and sometimes require our fear. What great thing has been born without fear, after all? When the shadow comes creeping, this is our prayer.

A shadow creeps close now. From out of the woods, he crawls. Faceless, he is, and without a name, but I see the twist of his horns when I find myself lost in my most haunted underworld. I hear his whispers when I'm left without my armored protectors, and I leave him offerings of milk and jewels on the mound. Should he find me, I know an initiation is nigh. Should I dare to take his dark hood down and dance with him, I just may hear the song I call my muse. To the shadowed one, I say come close. I am ready.

### 5.4. Song of the Pandemic Children
*When Trickster Visits the World*

The innocents have much to teach us. Young people have a brilliant way of illuminating what does not make sense about our world; their questions are our questions, if we dare ask them, and we must not discount their skepticism over our crumbling systems. Sometimes, they see what we can no longer see.

You, dear child, are extraordinary. Your courageous soul chose to descend just when a small, spiked trickster visited the world. You were born just as the old story ended, just as everyone stopped, struck by wonder and strange imaginings about work, kinship, death, and community. How brave you are, you bold, bold babe, for you shall surely see a most majestic age rise once this wild dance of birth ends in a well-timed stillness, a once-and-always gesture of human relatedness. Your song is my song, little one, and I will learn to sing it with you before I take my last breath.

### 5.5. The Quiet Monster
*To Whisper When Fear Is Afoot*

The inner trickster knows that sometimes what we fear most about our purpose, about being seen and having our creative gifts witnessed, is in fact our ultimate destination. The relationship between our fear and our most sacred work in the world can teach us much about our fate, and when fear's fangs bite into us before sleep, this is our prayer.

My fear is a quiet monster only I can hear, but that wily beast is getting too comfortable inside my heart. He sleeps during the day, I think, for I mostly sense his stirring after sundown. On the worst evenings, he haunts the space between awake and asleep, gnawing on his cage bars and chanting disharmonious rhymes of doom and gloom. Tonight, I say, *No more.* Tonight, I say to this creature: *Be still. I will listen when the time is right. I will grant you an hour to speak your mind when my body's tended and my strength's returned. For now, I must sleep, and so must bid you good night, dear beast. Leave my dreams be.*

## 5.6. The White Wolf and the Wildflowers
### *A Prayer-Story for Wolf-Women and Wild Kings*

Fairy tales are dance halls where our shadows waltz with our shape-shifters. These wonder stories house all our strangest parts and allow them to meet, love, sting, and change each other. Whereas our Western psychology narrows its lens and shines a spotlight on a single aspect of our story, surgically removing pieces of our psyche in order to pathologize, examine, and diagnose, fairy tales permit a more holistic plot to unfold where no character finds meaning in a vacuum, where every tension and twist is dependent upon another action. To that end, fairy tales are devotionals, medicinal prayers to the god of our own wholeness. When you work with a fairy tale, as when you work with a telling dream, consider all characters to represent a part of you and all plot points to reflect an aspect of your journey.

"The White Wolf," "Le Loup Blanc," is a French fairy tale that honors a common theme: the beastly, animal groom. These stories honor the initiatory experience of wedding the wild soul, of sacrificing a more polished life for one that is apparently less civilized, foreign, and, by extension, otherworldly. Allow this story to be a prayer to your own untamed nature. Notice where the plotlines of your life meet the story's unfolding, and name the questions that remain after you finish reading; often you'll find these are somehow the very questions of your life.

Once in a time before time, there lived and breathed a king, a queen, and their three daughters. Our story begins in those liminal hours when the sun is scarce, when the longest night has passed and the world is seeking out telling omens for the coming year. Hard times had befallen the kingdom, and the royal family's faith in their enduring wealth was fading quickly. Nevertheless, though the days were still quite short, the promise of warmer hours stirred the dream visions of all who dared to believe in better times.

None were more hopeful than the youngest of the princesses, though even she had begun to feel a mounting despair as the family's bounty wore thin. There were holes in the silk gowns and water in the whiskey. All three daughters had been raised to believe that their worth lay in their wealth and their name, and they would be able to marry for love. The name was still good, for now, but the wealth was all but gone, and on the edge of the new year, the daughters were realizing their family's only hope was for them to marry prosperous nobles or foreign kings. Needless to say, sorrow struck the hearts of them all.

The snows were deep in the kingdom this Yule, but the king was determined to attend the annual solstice hunt despite his ill fortune; this was for two reasons. Most notably, the king did not want others to know of his troubles, and his absence from the hunt would invite gossip. The winner of the hunt was also awarded a small cash prize, and the king could use all the liquid money he could get these days.

It was to be a long journey, and he would not return to see his queen and daughters for nine days' time. As he readied his horse, his soul welled with guilt. His daughters were with him, and their once-joyous faces seemed so melancholy. He decided there and then that, should he win the hunt and the money, he would spend it all on a gift for his girls.

"Tell me, dear daughters," he said, mounting his horse. "What can your father bring you that will grant you a sense of hope?"

"Well, Father," the oldest daughter answered first. "I would very much like a necklace with beads of quartz, rubies, diamonds, and sapphires."

The king nodded, a bit disappointed. The prize surely would be insufficient to afford such a necklace. "Perhaps I can find a necklace with quartz, yes."

"And I, dear Father," started the middle daughter, "would just love the brightest yellow dress stitched with gold thread and woven from the finest silk."

"A yellow dress, yes," the king amended.

Sighing, the king nodded and turned to the youngest daughter just as a heavy snow began to fall.

"What would bring me hope, Father ..." she hesitated. "What always brings me hope is seeing the world's wild beauty, noticing all that will remain even after our grand castle falls to ruins."

The older sisters rolled their eyes, and the king seemed bemused.

"Why, just last night, I dreamt of a wildflower crown. If you could bring me a crown of brightly blooming wildflowers, just as it was in my dream, gloriously braided and full of cherry and heather blossoms, with one great, blooming sunflower in the middle …" She was smiling, lost in her own wish now. "Well, that would most certainly bring me hope."

The winds were blowing now, and the king knew no wildflowers would bloom for months in these mountains, but he always loved a challenge.

"All right, my sweet daughters. Be good to your mother, and I will return with what you ask."

Into the storm he rode, accompanied by his men, all of whom were under strict orders to be on the lookout for any wildflowers peeking out through the ice and snow. None could be found, of course, but as soon as he made it to his destination, there was a trader who had a trunk full of treasures, including a quartz and garnet necklace and a garish yellow gown. The king acquired these for his oldest two daughters and felt foolish when he asked the trader, "Um, do you happen to have any wildflowers in that trunk?"

The trader scoffed, took his money, and waved the king away, the first of many moments of embarrassment the royal would have on this trip. Though the king was ordinarily quite skilled at hunting, for the whole of his time in the woodlands, he was so distracted by his search for wildflowers that the wild boar crossed his path many times but remained unscathed. The other kings and nobles on the hunt started to whisper that the king was not well, and the gossip he'd been hoping to avoid by attending the hunt followed him anyway.

The hunt ended without the king slaying any beasts, and though he had the gifts his elder daughters had requested, he had nothing for his youngest, the innocent who was always full of whimsy and wonder, his favorite daughter, truth be told. On the road back home, he lamented his many defeats, his inability to find flowers — something that cost nothing — somehow becoming a symbol of every unmet dream, every promise he'd broken, every failed opportunity to provide for his family he'd experienced in his long life. He began to weep, his men tried to console him, and the king considered not going home until the snows had melted a bit, until he could at least bring his daughter one, lone flower if not a whole crown.

In that moment of looming desperation, as it often happens, the king was met by the Otherworld. He stopped, staring into a pale mist that seemed to puff into and out of existence on the road. Sometimes, we can see clearly only what we expect to see, and this is why the Otherworld so often escapes our attention. If we hold the tension of the strange vision long enough, as the king did, we just might see the mythic standing before us.

After hours of being still on the road and staring into that mist, the king and his men saw it. There, on the road in front of them, stood a great white wolf. A massive creature, it was. The men begged the king to stop, but the king saw something they could not. He dismounted his fearful horse, and ignoring his men's pleas to not approach the wolf, the king crept closer to the wild one. As he did, he could see quite clearly that this wolf was wearing an exquisite crown of heather and cherry blossoms, woven so incredibly with ivy and grapevines, and, yes, there was even a great sunflower blooming at the center of the crown.

Grinning at the promise of bringing his youngest babe exactly what she asked for and against all odds, the king dared to speak to the wolf.

"Great wolf, I am the king of these lands, and I must have that crown you wear."

The wolf tilted its head and perked its ears.

"It's not for me but for the youngest princess, who asked for such a crown. I can offer you land, title, silver, gold, coins, gems ... whatever form you would like your riches to take, I can give them to you, for I am king."

The wolf sniffed, remained silent for a moment, bowed its head briefly to reveal the glory of the crown, then spoke: "I have no use at all for these things you offer, and in my thousands of years on this Earth, I have learned to never trust a king. A fickle lot, you are, and while your daughter sounds quite wise, I'm afraid you have nothing I need."

The king's heart fell into his stomach, and he wondered if he should order his men to kill the wolf, but something stopped him.

"That simply cannot be so," said the king. "I will not accept this. Everyone needs something, and if they don't, they certainly want something. Name your desire, wolf. Name it, and it shall be yours."

The wolf appeared to be thinking for a moment, narrowing his wide black eyes, but finally said, "All right, king. Here's my offer: I will give you this crown of wildflowers, and you will give me the very next living thing that meets you on the road. Whatever it is — be it a chipmunk or a songbird — capture it, and I will come to your castle in three days' time to collect what's mine. What do you say?"

The king frowned, surprised by the wolf's cryptic request, and thought for a moment. He wanted to refuse at first. After all, what if he was met by a human on the road, but he shunned this thought after a while. The snows were deep, and they hadn't passed anyone for miles. He was sure it would be a fox or a cat that crossed his path, and with the snow holding the tracks, his men could easily capture these small woodland creatures. Maybe a raven would fly overhead, and his men could easily hunt it with no leaves on the trees. The king could see no downside to this bargain, though one might say he hadn't thought hard enough.

In the end, he agreed, and the wolf disappeared. The wildflower crown was suddenly around the king's wrist, and though he had that nagging sense he had made a bad bargain nipping away at his insides, he focused intently on imagining his daughter's face when he gave her that wildflower crown, and this brought him immense joy.

He directed his men to be on the lookout for a creature — any creature at all, any living thing — on the final trek of their journey home. Though all the men and the king were vigilant, they saw nothing but snow. It was as if the land went dead. There was no wind, and the light went dim despite it being midday. There was no birdsong, no rustling in the brushes. The only breathing creatures on the road were the king and his men.

Soon, the castle was in view, and the king became quite nervous. Anyone could greet him at those gates, and a deal with the Otherworld was not a deal to be broken, he knew. He prayed. He willed a rabbit or a woodchuck to come out of hiding, but there was no one and nothing.

He thought about sending one of his men to bring a servant out. He thought about stopping right there until a bird flew overhead, but as soon as the thought entered his mind, the gates began to open. It was too late, and there, standing at the threshold to his grand house, was his youngest daughter, beaming with expectation.

"Oh," the king made a grief sound that did not match the princess's mood. "Oh, my daughter."

"Oh, Father!" she exclaimed, seeing the crown in the king's hands. "I never doubted you! Thank you so much! My heart is so full!"

The king could say nothing, knowing the fate that was to befall his daughter in three days, but he handed her the hard-won gift just the same. He left his men to give the gifts to his eldest daughters, locking himself away in his council room with the queen and telling her of his greatest folly. The two spent the whole of the night and most of the next day trying to think of a plan, and by sunset on the second day, the queen felt confident they could pass off one of the servant girls as the princess.

The white wolf arrived on the third day at dawn, as promised, and they had dressed the girl in the finest silk and given her the princess's jewels. The wolf was skeptical. After all, she was not wearing the crown of wildflowers, but he bade her climb on his back nonetheless.

Into the woods, they went, leaving the castle far behind.

"Where are we going?" asked the girl.

"To my house," answered the wolf, running swiftly through the wilds. After they had been traveling for half the day, the wolf slowed his pace. "We're nearly there now. Before I invite you into my home, why don't we take a little rest just here?"

The girl acceded, and the wolf stopped near a clear-running stream.

"Tell me," he started, "if this entire forest belonged to your father, what would he do with it?"

The girl thought for a moment, then answered, "Well, my father is quite poor. I imagine he would cut down some of these trees to build a fine house. He'd plant a small garden, collect water from this stream, and live quite well."

While the wolf was pleased with her answer, he now was sure this was not the princess. The king had betrayed him, as he thought he might, and he bid the girl climb onto his back at once.

"I apologize for taking so much of your time," the wolf said, running swiftly back to the castle. "I had mistaken you for the princess. When you return to the castle grounds, tell your father and mother they may travel here if they wish, find a plot of land, and build that house. May they live well, and may this forest, my forest, sustain them for many years to come."

It was long past sunset by the time they returned to the castle, and the king and queen were watching the wolf's approach, knowing their ruse had been uncovered. With many tears, they brought their youngest daughter down to meet the wolf, explaining the bargain, and when the wolf saw her, he knew immediately that she was the true daughter of the king. A crown of wildflowers, she wore, and she had the look of an innocent royal.

She said goodbye to her parents and sisters, shedding just one, lone tear for her life at the castle, and climbed atop the white wolf's back. All night they traveled, the princess sleeping on the wolf's back, and by dawn, the girl woke to find herself at the gates of a castle even grander than her father's, a castle that seemed to be made of bone.

"What is this place?" she asked, marveling at the intricately carved pillars and strong walls.

As soon as the gate opened, as soon as they crossed the threshold, the white wolf began to shiver, slowly dropping its fur. The princess was frightened and dismounted his back, and the wolf's spine straightened. His snout shrank, and in only a few breaths he was wolf no more. He had become a tall and strong youth, a wild king with kind eyes and scarred skin.

The princess quite liked the look of him, for his human eyes matched his creaturely eyes; full of story, shadow, and wolf song, they were.

"Am I to stay here with you, for the whole of my life?" the princess asked, and the shape-shifter's face softened a bit, for he could hear the sorrow in her question.

"You are free to leave whenever you wish," he answered, adding, "but I do hope you find something you seek here, something your deep soul desires."

The princess agreed to stay for one year, and when the next full January moon swelled, she would decide whether to stay or go.

She found the wolf's house to be quite wondrous, full of peculiar chambers where the art would come alive at midnight and secret archives where hidden histories were kept. She found herself staying up all night exploring this castle made of bone and its lush, untamed grounds. By the dawn of spring, she knew she had fallen in love with this wild place. By the longest day, she knew she had fallen in love with this wild king, this white wolf, this shape-shifter who spoke the language of the Otherworld. He made her laugh, and together they shared stories, food, and a simple life lived closed to the land.

She learned that the Wolf King had been enchanted long ago, in a time before there was time, and that he could be safe in his human form only while inside the walls of the bone castle. He kept his white wolf pelt hanging near the gate, and whenever he would leave, he would stretch the pelt over his back and wolf he would be once more. If he removed his pelt outside the castle walls, someone might steal it, cursing the forest to wither and its waters to run dry. He was the beating heart of these lands, you see. He was every ancient oak and night owl, every moss-kissed stone and mushroom. This was a spell that could not be broken, a spell of fate, a story written on the Wolf King's soul.

Before the first winds of autumn swept in from the west, the maiden began to feel whole in a way she never had before. Without the worries of her family's legacy or the duties of her name, she had somehow shed the vows that bound her, the vows she never took. In the castle made of bone and on these haunted lands, she was truly free.

"It's nearly been a year," the Wolf King said as they held one another beneath November's full moon. "Tell me, have you decided to stay? If so, would you do me the grand honor of becoming my bride?"

With hearts spilling over with joy and the last moon of autumn pouring silver light on their skin, the two made plans to be wed, but first they would need to journey back to her childhood home. Her eldest sister was to be married on the winter solstice, and the maiden who had found so much of what she never knew she needed in this strange place where nothing and everything made sense still longed for her sisters' faces, her father's kind words, and her mother's sharp wisdom.

The Wolf King gave her careful instructions meant to keep them both safe: "At midnight, you will hear me howl. This is my call, my warning we must begin our journey home. I won't want to leave without you, but I cannot stay past midnight. I may howl once, twice, or even three times, but never more than three. Without me, you will not find your way back to our castle made of bone. The way is hidden and always changing; only I can sense the way."

The journey through the forest as the snows fell was familiar, as the maiden rode on the back of the white wolf. She recalled how oddly comfortable she felt when she traveled through this same forest one year before on the wolf's back, and she understood now that her request for the wildflower crown, her father's bargain, and all the moments that had brought them together were the stuff of fate. She was living the life she was meant to live, and when she returned to her family, she showed them her happiness.

Her sisters understood and shared her joy. After some convincing, her father accepted that she was happy with the Wolf King, though his eyes were still full of guilt. It was the maiden's mother who refused to accept that her daughter could be happy with such a life, with such a beast for a husband.

"You must delay the wedding just a bit longer, dear daughter," the mother said just before the midnight howl came to call her daughter away. "It's in poor taste for you to marry before your middle sister, but do not worry, for she is to be wed in one year's time. Return to the castle next Yule, and after that, your father and I will be very happy to see you wed to ... your wolf."

Reluctantly, the maiden agreed. She would not marry the Wolf King yet. She would wait for her sister to marry, but she would spend that year as she had otherwise planned, in love with her wild wolf and at home in the castle made of bone. When midnight struck, she heard the howl of her betrothed, met him at the gate, and journeyed home.

While the two lovers spent the next four seasons falling more deeply in love with each other and the world, the maiden's mother spent that year planning. So vexed was she by her daughter's rogue ways, she stayed awake at night considering how she might break this terrible bargain, but the king could never go back on his word. With their wealth waning more and more every day, their name and reputation were soon to be all they had left.

Some say the answer came to the queen in a dream. Some say she consulted a Witch. Either way, before the wedding plans for her middle daughter had begun, she knew how she was going to rid her youngest of her wild king forever.

When the wheel of the year turned to the longest night once more, the castle was alive with many guests, music, and a bounty of inexpensive food disguised as luxuries. The Wolf King and the maiden arrived with the other guests and enjoyed the ceremony and the feasting. As he had done the previous year, the white wolf had told the maiden to listen for his midnight howl, to not miss it, and to come swiftly lest she could never return to their home.

As the hour grew late, the queen offered her daughter a drink, a glass of wine brewed with a sleep tonic, and the maiden fell into a deep sleep. When midnight came and her Wolf King howled for her, she was lost in the dreaming time. He howled, and he howled again, but his love did not come to the gate to meet him. He tried to find her before it was too late, running from room to room, catching her scent, refusing to believe she had betrayed him, but every room he searched was empty except the last one.

There by a quiet fire was the queen, a look of victory on her face, his great love sleeping on the cold stone floor.

"Oh, wolf," she clicked her tongue. "You do love my daughter, it appears. Alas, I cannot let my youngest child be married to a beast."

The Wolf King's body was growing weak, for he needed to return home. If he didn't leave that very instant, he was going to succumb to his humanity. He lay on the ground and begged, "Please. Return her to me."

The queen smiled, and it all happened at once then: The Wolf King shape-shifted, his spine straightening and his limbs growing long. His pelt lay on the floor, and the queen snatched it from the ground and tossed it in the fire. The Wolf King howled in great pain, a sound so tragic it shook the castle's walls and beckoned a great storm to come. Lightning struck the castle from all sides, and the thunder cracked and rolled. The walls began to crumble to the ground in great chunks of stone.

The wild king suddenly found himself returned to his castle made of bone, but his pelt was lost. He could never leave the grounds again, and his beloved forest was doomed to crumble and lie forever fallow. He wept in his grief, in his great and unnamable loss.

When the late dawn arrived, the maiden woke to find her old life in ruins all around her. The castle, her childhood home, was broken and full of bones. At the center of it all burned a fire in a hearth that still stood, the last remnant of the grand house. She knelt to warm herself there, and in the flames she saw the white wolf pelt, unburned, nested safely inside the dancing fire. The wild skin was untouched, not one hair singed.

She pulled it from the fire and stretched it around her shoulders. She knew nothing of what had happened the night before, and she held hope that her Wild King did not believe she had betrayed him. Remembering his words, she was determined to find her love no matter what it might take. Surely, there had to be a way. In that moment, she looked to the sky and howled the howl of the wild soul, the sound that stirs the deep self awake, and she walked along the haunted road, leaving her childhood behind forever.

She tried to remember the way, but she had always been sleeping when they traveled the stretch of road between the wolf's forest and her father's land. She knew it should take about half a day, but it was nearly nightfall now, and she could still see the smoking ruins of her father's castle behind her in the east. No matter how far she walked, she was still so close to her old home. No matter how hard she wished for her Wolf King to find her, she was alone in these woods.

It was dark now, and the maiden pulled the pelt close to keep warm as the snows fell. A great north wind came, whistling in her ear, and she thought she heard a song in the sound. She asked the wind out loud, "Have you seen the wolf?" and the wind whispered back, "Noooo."

The maiden kept walking, the snow stopped falling, and the stars began to shine. She asked the stars, "Have you seen the wolf?" and the stars twinkled and drummed, "No, no, no."

Nearly dawn it was now, and the sun was rising behind her. She looked back and could no longer see the smoke from the old castle's ruins. As a pale sun rose on the horizon, she asked the sun, "Have you seen my Wild King?" and the sun said, "Keep going."

The maiden's feet were frozen now. Her eyelashes carried snowflakes, and her hair hung in icicles. Still, she pressed on. When she felt she could go no farther, she sat in the snow, pulled the pelt over her head, and howled just as the moon rose. This time, she heard a howl in return. Again, she howled, and again, the sound was echoed.

She asked the moon, "Have you seen the Wolf King?" and the moon said, "Yes." The maiden was running on all fours now. She could see in the dark. She had a new name, and there in the shadows stretched the castle made of bone. The wildflower crown hung on the gate, and she placed it atop her head just as the gate groaned open.

Her Wild King stood at the threshold with outstretched arms. When he saw his great love and his wolf pelt, the Wild King knew all would be well. The land would stay green and growing, the waters would keep flowing, and soon the wildflowers would be in full bloom once more. The wild pelt hung on the inside of the gate near the wildflower crown, and the two became one. When the days were warm again, the maiden married the wild one beneath a spring moon, each wearing crowns of heather flower and cherry blossom, each with a wolf-fur pelt around their shoulders, each living happily ever after, made so, as we all are, by both gratitude and grief.

## 5.7. My Wolf King and Me
*To Honor an Untamed Rite of Passage*

Long ago, I met a Wolf King on the road who promised to gift me a wilder life. He wore a crown woven from hope, and he tricked my strongest protectors into believing he was a harmless fool. My wiser soul saw him for what he was, I think. Some cunning part of me that grew weary of the old wars bade my inner warrioress lay down her sword, and I let him carry me through the borderlands to his castle made of bone. There, I named my wild innocence home, and I let my civilized world crumble to dust around us, my Wolf King and me. In time, I wore that wild pelt as my own, and I let my soul's skin terrify the tame one I used to be.

## 5.8. Morning Prayer of the Maker
*To Inspire the Artist's Diamond-and-Worm Soul*

The trickster requires timelessness. In the old stories, when the trickster is near, time stops. Often, there is a choice to be made that requires the same intuitive presence an artist knows well, a choice that demands a surrender to deep time. Deadlines can be the enemy of inspiration, we know. If our muse is sourced from the Otherworld and trickster energy is required for creation, then the maker must orient themselves toward a certain timelessness, an intentional losing of time's linear direction. In these moments, this is our prayer.

Oh! I'm waking wild today! I'm suddenly unbound by the chains of linear time, and I'm living whole and luscious lifetimes in the space between my inhale and exhale. I'm befriending the most curious possibilities and making art as if I've never met a clock or a calendar. My soul is full of worms and gold, muck and diamonds, wound and treasure, in equal parts, and I'm weaving a grand tapestry from my many splendid contradictions. On this, the morning of all mornings, may I create as if I were the first and last human to live on this holy, wild rock called Earth, as if art were the first and last savior of this planet.

## 5.9. You Are No Coyote
*To Howl at Lying Kings*

We live in an age when the power hungry wear coyote pelts and dare to tread in the footprints of the trickster, but tricksters they are not. The trickster despises the spotlight, after all. An idea that would be accepted by the masses does not disturb the world story in ways the trickster requires, and as every Witch knows, a truly disruptive spell must be cast inside the hidden cave, not from any stage.

Fancy yourself a trickster, do you? I might wonder, then: Why did I see you coming from a million miles away, wearing a fox skin and demanding attention? A true trickster knows the power of the shadows and is well versed in the art of invisibility. They have a clever tongue and wield it well. You won't find them on a stage boasting about their boons, and, my dear sir, you most certainly won't see them preaching from a podium before the prayerful masses. If given the choice, a trickster would always choose change over fame, art over fortune. A good story could never unfold without them, but, my poor king, I'm afraid my story will continue in your absence without any holes in the plot. You are no coyote, not even a one-trick pony, and I hope you meet a real trickster on this haunted road who might show you a thing or two about the Otherworld.

## 5.10. The Naked Fawn
### *To Remember in Embarrassing Moments*

If we dare to revisit our most embarrassing moments, we just might find fate's thread buried there. What patterns exist in those troublesome memories that flush your cheeks and quicken the heart, those bizarre moments that are somehow, strangely, neither regrets nor woundings? Often these patterns can orient us toward our souls' deepest truths, illuminating the clash between how we wish to be seen and how we are seen, showing us the rough edges we scrape against when we are close to that wild thing called purpose.

Could I crawl into the darker-than-dark corner of a secret sea cave, I would. Could I hide my flushed cheeks and wet eyes behind an ice mask and never speak of this again, I would. Tonight, the memory of the moment is loud, and I am a naked fawn trembling in a treeless field. It's open season on my pride, and when my heart slows its terrible rhythm, I shall remember the miracle of these harsh encounters when my inner protectors failed me, when a small misunderstanding becomes a great teacher, when my better maps prove false and my trusted lanterns burn out. Here, I seek the space between who I believe myself to be and who I am beneath this Witch warrior's armor; may I curl up there and laugh-cry myself to sleep.

## 5.11. Ode to the Trickster
### *For Those Losing Faith in Their Art*

Do not lose heart, maker, for the whole world is brewed by your hands. When the madness is great, when the soup has spilled and the recipes are lost, when the paint cans are empty and the page is full of senseless scribblings, may you remember that birth follows chaos. Keep going.

## 5.12. The Terror Teacher
### *To Whisper after a Nightmare*

Sometimes, a nightmare is an uninvited but timely visitor. When a beastly dream wakes us to a dark room full of old ghosts and creeping shadows, we let our heart-drums slow to a soft, midnight rhythm. We breathe. We ask the questions only a dreamer can ask: What does this shadow dream have to show me? What can I learn from the faceless phantoms who haunted me in that terror-scape built by my mind? What prophecy lies therein? Sometimes, the answers are in the dream's missing pieces, the pages torn from the Book of Nightmares by our inner protectors.

To these fighting men who roam the psyche in search of medicine that might be too bitter, I say let me see it all. Hide nothing from me, lest this dream return to hex my peaceful midnight yet again. May I learn from these terror teachers now, right now before the dawn takes my will, before the sun steals my storied memory of the dreaming time. Gather the missing pages. Dig them from the deep cracks in my certainty, for surely I am ready to see what wants to be healed from this self-curated gallery of horrors. Surely I am ready to see what lurks in the secret corners of my dreamer's mind, what lies in wait behind the well-polished furniture inside the haunted mansion of my heart.

## 5.13. Gifts of Lead and Gold
### *The Alchemical Brilliance of These Times*

This world keeps a secret from us, I think, and perhaps it must be so. Somewhere, in a time long gone that still is, a holy one made gold from lead, a treasure from the muck. Housed in the hollow of every belly is an echo of that hooded alchemist, willing the wound to shine. The mage bids we see the brilliance of what bleeds inside the seat of our soul, the bounty buried in the rot. Our great gift can kill us as easily as it can save us, after all. Our art hurts as it heals, and such is the alchemical brilliance of these times. May we build twin altars to the lead and the gold, naming the gifter's ache as sacred as the gift itself.

# *6*

# THE BOOK OF THE MOUNTAIN MAGE

### *Prayers for Sacred Solitude, Transformation, and Inner Alchemy*

*The archetype of the mage* invites visions of long staffs raised over crystalline orbs, of hooded Pagans with long beards and longer memories. Our inner mage is a great transformer, an immortal alchemist who finds meaning in witching a life into motion, in shocking awake the sleeping soul. The prayers of the mage are prayers to the unseen others, to nature's invisible intelligence that resources our wants and sees the spell to fruition.

Imagine the prayers in The Book of the Mountain Mage spoken by a hooded pyromancer tending a fire on a wild mountaintop. They pray to find magick in the mundane moments, to will a vision into being and name real what is, as yet, only imagined. They invite the spirit of certainty to step into their body and animate their dreams, and they welcome a quiet, steadfast power home. These are their prayers and yours.

## 6.1. The Old Haunted Skin
### *The Snake's Dark Moon Eulogy*

Shedding this too-small skin, I am, for this serpentine queen must make herself ready for what comes. Another way and a better day begin tomorrow, and as midnight befalls my sorrow, I am sloughing the haunted scales of old names and flaking regrets. I am crossing a threshold called renewal, and I will not return to collect my fallen corpse; though it looks like me, this skin is but a ghostly husk of who I once was but will never be again. Beneath this dark moon, I leave the old self behind. I repent nothing, and I welcome a wilder dawn.

## 6.2. In Praise of Our Wild Stories
*To Sing When the Moon Is New*

May this new moon call us closer to the deep medicine of our living myths, as we circle 'round the moss-and-leaf bed of a dying moon. Here, in the space of a lone breath, may we be beast, mist spirit, and maiden. May we be mage, fool, hag, handless daughter, and wild king. May we be witness to the Pagan poetry of our lives, these peculiar evening hours, becoming a living ghost story just as the sun sets on our tamer ways. Here, we leave a song in the mud as the dying moon takes its last breaths, as the new moon gifts us a heathen hymn to sing the old one's soul home.

## 6.3. Readying a Room
*To Remember in Mundane Moments*

The mage understands we must make ourselves a hospitable environment for the world we wish to see bloom to fruition. We must prepare a room for what we desire and leave the door open for the magick to visit.

This mundane morning seems to have lost its magick, but this Witch knows there is an otherworldly order afoot. Something wild this way comes, and I'm readying a room for this miracle.

## 6.4. Some Small Spirit
*To Name the Mundane Holy*

If I dare to stare long enough into my teacup, I just might witness my own fate. I just might see a glimmer of clarity in the crystals of the honey drop perched on the rim. I might see a misty shape hidden in the depths of this mundane medicine, some small spirit come to gift me with a grand knowing found in the humblest place: there is already a version of me cackling with unnamable joy under a haunted summer moon, and they are singing mad songs of blessing just for me, their most incredible memory, the Witch who sips her tea.

## 6.5. In the Muses' Cave
### *When the Evening Goes Quiet*

The old stories say the muse never dances in the sunlight but dwells deep in the underground. Here, in the wells, foxholes, and caves, a soft fire is tended by a hag who knows no glamour. In a rough and rolling voice, she speaks of an art that can be born only in the dark, only in the secret cocoons and subterranean caverns where unnamed rivers flow. When the evening goes quiet, I know how to find this place. I recover the map to the muses' cave from the forbidden underground and set out to find a forgotten magick. Wait for me.

## 6.6. Left Alone at the Fire Temple
### *For the Fawning Times*

Even the best of us may fall at the feet of another, naming a teacher god or a friend savior. These are the fawning times, fleeting moments of seeing our own shining self mirrored in the face of another human creature, a soft-skinned animal who breathes as we breathe but seems to be an angel. If we refuse to let these moments have their way with us, these aching encounters can be healing portals, rare opportunities to amplify our art and recover our own power, having seen a glimmer of who we are becoming in another's eyes.

May I see this moment as a timely invitation to tend my own gifts, to venture to the fire temple in solitude and stoke the flames of my inner vitality. Here, as the altar candles burn, I will take stock of my own strength. In the hearth, I will see the shine of my own sun. There, in that heathen church, I'll stay. Only when my eyes are alight with the stellar fusion of inspiration will I leave. Only when I've remembered my true name and spoken with the old ghosts will I return, and when I do, may my golden fire be witnessed by the world.

## 6.7. Drumming the Obstacles to Death
### *To Empower a Spell to Fruition*

Live, live, live, I say. The circle is cast, the old gods are close, and I, this tough-boned Witch, am willing this vision to breathe. The mountain dwellers of the north are here, rooting my desire deep through miles of mud and stone. The choir of winged ones who live inside the eastern dawn are here, gracing this want with their glory. The hot-fleshed fire dancers of the south who speak the language of the snakes are here, licking this spell with forked tongues and drumming the obstacles to death, and the hooded sea hags of the west are here, howling their salty songs and cocooning this vision in a wild bundle of shell and kelp. So we will it, so it shall be, and the vision takes its first inhale. Live, live, live. And so it is.

## 6.8. Our Heathen Home
### *To Remember When the Sun Sets on Our Screens*

The moon is rising above our heathen home now, and the sun is setting on our many screens. Just for now, let us know the beauty that can be witnessed only here, only by the quiet light of a new moon. Just look at her; she's a silver-tongued poetess wearing a ball gown of wild intentions, starlight, and ancient memories. May she spill seeds of Pagan poetry into our dreams, gifting us with the long-vision, with muse, with lunar inspiration that waxes and wanes, that swells to fruition when we see beauty in the rot of these times. May we be awestruck by that holy 'twixt-and-'tween place where the barren treetops meet a violet sky, where the mystical autumn dusk meets the healing darkness of our heathen home.

## 6.9. Stay Out at Sea
*A Petition to Send a Storm Away*

The torrent comes, and the wilds are ready. The birds have left, and the wolves have gone to higher ground. Alas, there are those soft-fleshed creatures who cannot go, whose lives are threatened by these winds and waters. For them, I petition this storm to stay out at sea. I bid the elementals who speak the language of the invisible currents carry the storm's eye away from these shores, and I become a foulmouthed tempest and a living squall. Hear me and go, you wild mother. My breath sets the change in motion, and out to sea you go. Away!

## 6.10. The Mage's Rocking Chair
*A Song of Radical Rest*

Where our capitalist overculture demands endless production and consumption, rest is revolution. Importantly, rest does not mean stillness for everyone. We rest in ways that make the hours meander instead of race. We rest to live slowly, to resist the rush, and to name holy that sense of timelessness that greets us when we consciously invoke the mage's presence.

Just for today, I am naming rest the stuff of rebellion. My voice needs to sleep if it is to scream. My eyes must witness the small and sweet if they are to see the horrors of these times. My body wants stillness in order to better fight. Tomorrow, I may wake reborn and carry those weighted scales of justice through the hours, but for today, I am sinking into the rhythm of my mage's rocking chair. I cast no spells, save the spell of quietude. I raise neither wand nor sword, neither hex nor healing libation. I am full of questions and empty of answers, slow-rocking the day away and dreaming strange futures into being, one breath at a time.

## 6.11. Amber Honey, Hearth, and Her-Story
*A Pyromancer's Prayer*

I am lost in the amber-honey flames of my heathen imaginings on this, a most tender evening. Here, I pray into the fires of my mind. I invite the soothing spirit of a memory to find me now, as I wonder about the lost her-stories we will never study, as I hold the tension of these times under my tongue. May I be marked by a healing moment here, some spark of time I might call *past*, though I know better, a slow-burning memory that met me long ago and never left the hearth of my soul's home. Tonight, I name this memory the medicine, the cooling salve, for the Witch's burn. May I breathe deep here, and may I be resourced by the wisdom of my more innocent days.

## 6.12. Matters of Mayhem and Trust
*To Speak in Times of Transition*

The hours of the night are numbered now, and my sleep was spent at the sacred well where I go to find answers. I know not what will become of me, as my concern turns to matters of mayhem and trust. These are transitional times. As my tired eyes blink open, I stand on the bridge between what was and what will be, and I sing.

## 6.13. Holy Howls
*To Sing When the Moon Is Full*

This full moon is made of holy howls, longing, and silver fire, stitched together by that wise and wicked thread of fate. May we wander long in its ghostly glow this midwinter evening when the certainties are few and the curiosities are many. Here, we are creaturely, hunting a new dream in the shadows of these haunted snowscapes, tracking the older-than-ancient footprints of the Cailleach back through the ice caves of deep time. Lost in these heathen imaginings, may we welcome our next once-upon-a-time. May we sense a new story and sniff out a hidden path, readying our dream den for its ceremonial thaw, naming truth treasure and finding food for the spirit in winter's befuddlement, in these dark and wild fallows.

∽◦◠

# 7

# THE BOOK OF THE WOUNDED HEALER

*Prayers for Heartache, Healing,
and the Shining Self*

*The wounds of our world* require a rich apothecary of archetypal medicines, but if there is one archetype — one "original form" — that might carry the most potent salve for humanity's scorched skin, it is the wounded healer. They walk with a limp, bearing the wounds of their childhood and the scars left on their skin by a fate they did not choose, yet they hold a wealth of healing knowledge unmatched by those who claim to be fully healed and fully well. They share their wisdom with those who care to listen, who do not dismiss a healer because they see them bleeding.

We all house a great wound and a sacred treasure, our muck and our gift, inside our souls. When the wound aches, our healer's jewel aches, too. A healer-teacher who claims a purity of being, who boasts complete and infallible wholeness, is likely hiding a terrible wound of the spirit. Conversely, someone who claims only woundedness, who is always seeking medicine from someone they deem more whole than themselves, has had their treasure buried so long that they've forgotten where they hid that gold.

A wounded healer does not wish to sever the ache from the medicine. They understand that their inner treasure is made more valuable because of their wound, and their wound bleeds when others bear witness to their gift. Unfortunately, in a world where a fickle hero called capitalism shapes our systems, the wounded-healer archetype can become so easily deformed. We see this when trauma becomes monetized instead of made into art for art's sake. We see those new on their own healing paths claim to be wise wayfinders. We see old healing traditions commodified, trademarked, and degraded, and we forget to look for the old healer hag who limps alongside the road.

The prayers in The Book of the Wounded Healer are spoken by her, that medicine keeper. You can't search her name online, and she won't call out to you while you pass her by. Look for her on the edges of your initiations, in the hushed whispers you heard in the underworld when the night was long. Listen for her while you walk through the dusty archives of your story. When you were abandoned and left adrift in the initiatory sea, whose song brought you comfort? When you were full of faith in a trusted friend who removed their mask to reveal the face of a betrayer, who walked you home? Look to the patterns in your most medicinal moments, and you will surely find the wounded healer there. These are her prayers and yours.

## 7.1. The Medicine Bag She Carries
### *Song of the Old Healer Hag*

Full of stones, stories, and broken dreams, that old bundle is. Swollen with bones, grief song, and spells, her medicine bag seems more burden than gift these days when the wounds are many and the healers are few. Even so, that old hag carries it well, walking the rough landscapes of these times, humming her way through the protests on the streets and the hospital halls. You can find her if you look; she's there. Give her a nod and a wink. Leave her a grateful note with some honeyed tea so her song can go on. Teach others to listen for her healing hymn when the days are dark, for her quiet harmony carries a medicine made for us all.

## 7.2. Though My Skin Is New
*When the Old Wound Bleeds*

This old wound still bleeds, though my skin is new. It's become a part of me, I think, and I'm using the blood to paint a storyboard full of miracles for this, my newly imagined life.

## 7.3. Together, We Shine
*To Awaken a Hidden Gift*

Some innate gifts are inherited from the ancestors, and these shimmering treasures become lighthouses as we age, sweeping beacons orienting us toward what is for us and away from the rocks that wreck. In time, if we dare to dive deep below the rough surface of who we know ourselves to be, we find even greater treasure, a long-submerged bounty inherited from the Fates; these are the treasures that terrify, the boons bestowed by the bone-women who weave the world. We have no pattern for these soul-destined wonders, no hero with a great name to show us how to invest these riches, no great patriarch to do the paperwork for us. Our shifting world often seems incompatible with these deeper gifts, and we may find great challenge in cultivating an art few will understand and many will reject, yet if we are fortunate enough to find our people, to unlock the treasure chest before them and bid them bear witness to our unnamable wealth, we may find there is no greater reward in this life.

Today, many ears will hear my soul song, but I shall sing for the ones who listen with their hearts, who sense strange harmonies in my hymn and find themselves suddenly home in my most sacred sound. I awaken my hidden gift this day, and I bid others do the same. Together, may we make a borderless world full of neighborly chatter, community gardens, and curious children. Together, we shine.

## 7.4. The Medicine of Memory
### *A Healing Prayer-Song When Sickness Strikes*

This medicinal moon is singing me a honey-tongued healing song, a haunted hymn of hearth and harvest that brings me home to the wild truth of who I am when the dead scales of to-dos and must-haves flake and fall away from my fevered skin. Here, I breathe deeper in this exquisite and ephemeral flesh. I see a strange beauty in the waltz of birth and death, and I grant a rhythm to this eternal dance by my breath and the beat of my heart-drum. May I heal swiftly and well, finding a treasure in this fever dream, my eyes opening to wilder ways to be when the sickness is gone, when the healing morning dawns.

## 7.5. Gold Tree and Silver Tree
### *A Prayer-Story for the Shining Self*

Some stories show us the most extreme parts of ourselves, highlighting the wit and depravity of our inner annihilators and the stunning brilliance of our inner shining selves. We might follow a thread in our life stories that shows the wicked dance between these two characters. In some ways, our most sacred work is made from encounters between these two polarized sides of ourselves — the most wounded self and the most healed and gifted self.

Collected from the Scottish Highlands, "Gold Tree and Silver Tree" is a fairy tale that illuminates the dark side of the feminine, the shadow mother and her bloodlust for our inborn brilliance. As you read this gnarly prayer-story of femicide, divination, polyamory, and the hidden purpose of the deep soul, permit the old and young kings to represent your inner protectors, those who, despite their best efforts, often fail to keep the inner predators, your Silver Trees, at bay. Name the questions you still hold at the story's end and, perhaps, keep them on your altar for a time, noticing the ways in which the creaturely realm, dreams, and otherworldly experiences step forward and offer you strange answers.

Once in a time that was and was not, there lived a nameless king and his beloved queen, his Silver Tree. In time, as it happens, they had a daughter, a little innocent who they called Gold Tree. The mother's silver bark skin shone like the full moon's light, and the girl's gold bark skin glimmered like the sun on the longest day.

When Gold Tree was a babe, in the time of her curious youth, she spent many hours of every day with her beloved mother. Together, they would venture into the haunted forest and find the holy well, as Silver Tree's mother had also done with her when she was a girl, as her mother before her had done. A matrilineal pastime it was, to go into the woods on the day of the sun, stare into the well, and as legend directed, bid the spirit of the well rise up from the deep and speak prophecy.

Though the spirit of the well never revealed itself to Gold Tree and Silver Tree, they kept this ritual. They tended to their kinship on these days of joy and adventure, and their bond was strong. Gold Tree loved to sing, and she would hum spontaneous songs as they walked through all seasons, singing to the wildflowers when they bloomed in summer, the autumn leaves when they fell, the first frost crystals of winter on the moss, and the sparking seeds under the soil before spring's dawn. Mother and daughter were so close on these small journeys, and the love that can only be shared between mother and daughter grew in its strength, becoming all but impenetrable.

As Gold Tree grew older, though, her skin began to shine even brighter, and her voice grew loud. No one was sure why it happened exactly, but one day Silver Tree found herself annoyed by her daughter's singing; there was a power in the resonance she had not heard before, and in time, Gold Tree's songs began to give Silver Tree terrible headaches. The queen began avoiding her daughter in the halls, ceased having dinner with the family, and on the day of Gold Tree's first blood, began refusing to go on their weekly walks to the well.

The change was a mystery to all it affected. Gold Tree's young mind could not fathom why her loving mother was no longer spending time with her, and Silver Tree also was unsure of why her daughter was suddenly irksome. The nameless king, too, was befuddled, unsure of what strange fate was befalling his small family.

One morning, on Gold Tree's thirteenth birthday, Silver Tree woke to hear her daughter's singing, as she often did, but on this day, she was positively repulsed. She gagged, and she retched. Every note the girl sang churned her stomach in a different direction, and Silver Tree buried her head beneath pillows to muffle the sound. Alas, the song still got through the layers of fabric and down, and Silver Tree screamed in helpless despair, tearing down the hall and rushing out the door toward the haunted forest.

Perhaps it was out of spite that she was going to the well without her daughter, or perhaps there was some other divine providence afoot. Nevertheless, Silver Tree went to the well alone, gripped the edges of the ancient portal to the Otherworld, and wailed into the depths. So great was her cry, so fierce was her demand, that the spirit of the well had no choice but to respond and reveal itself.

The well's spirit was today taking the form of a little silver truth-telling trout. The fish erupted from the bowels of the earth and swam in quick clockwise circles in the water. Silver Tree was stunned but stayed steadfast in her desire to hear a certain prophecy. When her heart calmed enough to speak, the queen made her demands: "Little trout in the well, tell me: Who is the most shining one of all?"

The trout spun around once, then spoke. "You are, my queen. You, Silver Tree, are the most shining one of all."

The queen released a breath she didn't realize she was holding, and a weight seemed to be lifted from her back. She sighed with relief, nodded once, and returned to the castle. All seemed peaceful for a few years. The household formed a new peculiar dynamic, with Silver Tree tolerating her daughter from time to time. Their mother-daughter day journeys were no more, but they found they could again speak to one another. Silver Tree had no love left for her daughter, but she found a new tolerance for her Gold Tree's voice.

One summer night, a terrible vision crept into Silver Tree's dreams. Gold Tree was about to turn nineteen, the age of transformation, the cusp of womanhood, and Silver Tree dreamt of her daughter shining so brightly her light burned all it touched. Her face was brighter than the sun, and her song was so powerful it shook the world. Silver Tree woke and ran to the mirror, touching her dulling silver bark skin. The dream vision of Gold Tree's brilliance was vibrant in her mind, and her own light seemed so pale in comparison. She wept, then she raged, running from the castle before dawn broke and finding the well just as a wicked sun was rising.

"Little trout in the well!" Silver Tree wailed into the depths. "Who is the most shining one of all, this day?"

The spirit of the well heard the queen's cry and bubbled to the water's surface. Unable to lie, the trout answered truthfully, "The most shining one of all, this day, is your own daughter, the gleaming Gold Tree."

The well's words were full of horror for the queen, and she felt physical pain at their sound. She shook as if she'd been cut with a poisoned blade, and she howled in such terror that the haunted forest withered as if it were winter. She lay there at the base of the well for a time, watching the geese fly overhead and listening for the voice of a savior that never came. When the hour grew late, she began trudging home, wearing the weight of the trout's truth, and she took to her bed without speaking to anyone.

For two weeks, Silver Tree lay in her bed behind a locked door, occasionally sipping water but eating no food. Both Gold Tree and the nameless king would knock on the door from time to time, full of worry for their matriarch, but Silver Tree would send them away. Wallowing in the muck of self-pity, she was. With no one to pull her out, she stayed there in the slough.

Finally, in a far weakened state, Silver Tree let the king into her chambers. He sat at her bedside, held her hand, and shook with great grief, for his only love was surely dying.

"Tell me, my Silver Tree, my beauty," the king begged. "Tell me what I can do to heal you. I am king, after all. I can bring medicines from all over the world, but I must know what has brought you to this state. Please, my wife, my life, tell me what I can do."

Silver Tree said nothing, staring blankly out the window at the full moon. The king continued with his pleas, and finally, after many hours, Silver Tree whispered, "I will not tell you of my sickness, for you would never understand, but I will tell you what medicine I require."

"Yes! Yes!" The king lifted his head from his hands, his eyes alight. "Yes, anything. Tell me. I will bring it at once."

"I'm afraid, King..." Silver Tree hesitated. "I'm afraid you will not so readily procure this medicine for me, but I will tell you nonetheless."

"My queen, whatever will save your life, I vow I will find it for you."
He straightened his spine and readied himself, but no amount of resolve
would prepare him for what the queen would say.

"Very well." Silver Tree rolled her head to meet his gaze. "Within
three days, I must eat the heart and the liver of our daughter, Gold Tree.
If I do not, these days will be my last."

The king frowned, confused, then sorrowful, then full of anger.

"Silver Tree," he started, standing and pacing. "What madness is
this? Surely there must be another way. Our daughter need not die so
you can live; no god would will it so."

Silver Tree said no more and feigned sleep, leaving the king to decide which of his women he would save. He could scarcely sleep that
night, restless and full of fear, but when sleep did find him just before
dawn, he was given the gift of a telling dream. In the dream, he saw a
young foreign king, a good soul who was searching the world for his
own queen. When the old nameless king woke, he knew what he must
do, though he had to act very quickly.

He described the young king from his dream to his most trusted
council, and they told him this young king was, indeed, very real. In
secret, the old king arranged for his daughter to meet this foreign king,
and by dawn on the third day after Silver Tree had told the king what
medicine she required, Gold Tree was on a ship sailing to the foreign
king's castle. She had been told her mother was not well and had become quite dangerous, and she agreed that leaving her homeland was
better than staying in a place where she could never shine.

The old king put the heart and liver of a dying goat on a platter and
brought them to his queen. She devoured them raw and whole, and in
that moment, the old king was forever changed, for he saw the horror
of his queen. She leaped from her bed, suddenly whole and well, her
silver skin brighter than ever before and the look of a beast in her eyes.
He knew then, of course, that she had lied, for she had eaten neither the
heart, the vitality, nor the liver, the purity, of their daughter but was still
whole and well. He vowed to never speak of Gold Tree's whereabouts to
his queen, and he lived out the rest of his days with these secrets.

Gold Tree, in the house of the foreign king, was happier than she
had ever been. Every morning, she would rise, go to the balcony that

overlooked the sea, and sing. The rising sun would gleam and glimmer on her gold bark skin, and her voice would echo over the waves so every soul in the land could hear her song and witness her joy. Such wild gratitude did she wake with each day, and in time, she fell deeply in love with the king, who already loved her, his glorious, shining one.

Many years passed in this way, but one night, on the eve of Gold Tree's birthday, another dream came to visit Silver Tree. This dream was much like the nightmare that had vexed her so many years ago, sending her to the well and to her bed, but in this new dream, Gold Tree was shining like the sun in a foreign land where the sea was blue and the wind swept in from the south. Silver Tree woke and went to the well, demanding once more that the spirit of the well tell her who is the most shining one of all.

"It's Gold Tree, my queen," spoke the trout. "Your daughter, Gold Tree, still shines the brightest of them all."

"You lie!" Silver Tree snapped, spitting in the well and knocking an old stone into the water. "Gold Tree is dead."

The fish swam in a slow circle and said, "No, my queen. She is alive, well, and full of joy."

She howled into the well so loudly that the trees bent back, and she ran back to the castle with such speed that she carved a path in the ground. Finding the king alone in his study, she gripped him by the neck and snarled, "You lied to me, King."

Realizing his old secret had been uncovered, the king was silent for a moment, considering the state of things. Finally, he said, "And you lied to me, Silver Tree. You said it was only our daughter's heart and liver that could bring you health, but I fed you those of a goat, and you leaped from your bed as if you were full of youth. I lied to save our daughter, yes, but your lie was far worse, was it not?"

Silver Tree was seething now, and she struck the king with the back of her hand. He fell to the ground, and she demanded, "You tell me where she is, and I'll kill her quickly. If you don't tell me, I'll find her myself. You know I will, and her death will go on for years. You'll hear her screams in your sleep, and her pain will be on your head."

The old king blinked away tears, saying behind a sob, "What's become of you, Silver Tree?"

In the end, the old king did tell Silver Tree where their daughter was. That night, as the queen sailed south, the old king took his own life, hanging himself deep in the haunted forest and whispering words of apology to his dear daughter, his beloved shining one. The land spirits mourned that night, for he had been a good king who tended the wilds with great care, his choice of queen his only folly in an otherwise brilliant life.

As she always did, Gold Tree rose at dawn to sing, but on this morning, she saw an awful vision in the distance. At first it was not clear, but as she held her breath, she began to see the sun glinting off her mother's silver bark skin. Her mother was coming to kill her, she knew, and her king was away on a hunt.

She beseeched the servants to hide her in the cellar, inside the room with the red door, to lock her inside and give no one the key. The servants loved Gold Tree, so they did as they were told. Alas, just as our inner predators always know how to find our inner shining ones, Silver Tree knew exactly where Gold Tree was hiding. Arriving on the shore, she marched straight from the dock to the castle, down the stairs, and knocked on the red door.

"Oh, my dear Gold Tree," she started in a sweet voice. "They told me you were dead. I'm so happy to hear you are alive and well. Now, do come out. Let us have a proper mother-and-daughter reunion."

Gold Tree swallowed. She believed there was still something good inside her mother, still some part of that wild soul who guided her into the haunted forest, who loved to hear her soft songs, but she did not want to die.

"Oh, Mother, you're here," she started. "I'm afraid I'm locked in here, and only my husband holds the key. He's away hunting for another few days."

Silver Tree's face, if Gold Tree could have seen it, would have made her scream in terror, but she composed herself and calmed her voice. "Well, I'm afraid I can't wait for your king to arrive home, but I wonder: What if you could simply slip your smallest finger through the keyhole? I'll give it a kiss, and this will have to be our only reunion for now."

Gold Tree considered this, thinking there was little harm that could come from her mother's kiss on her pinkie finger but, more importantly, remembering how warm her mother's love once was.

"All right," Gold Tree obliged, holding her breath and slipping her finger through the keyhole.

In an instant, her mother pricked her finger with a poisoned silver thorn. Gold Tree pulled her hand back, but it was too late. She fell to the ground, lifeless.

Silver Tree, beaming with her victory, left the castle and sailed home. When she arrived there the next morning, she went straight to the well.

"Little trout in the well, tell me, who is the most shining one of all?"

The trout surfaced and swam in a swift circle, answering, much to the joy of Silver Tree, "You are, my queen. You, Silver Tree, are surely the most shining one of all."

Silver Tree breathed easy and even thanked the little fish, walking home slowly and reveling in her beauty.

Meanwhile, the young king arrived home from his hunt to find his great love dead behind the red door. So great was his grief, he lay there with her body for many moons. His servants brought him food and water, but he refused to leave the room with the red door. Some say he began to go a little mad, speaking to Gold Tree at night as if she were still alive. He refused to bury her, his shining one, for the sun does not belong underground.

One year after Gold Tree's death, on her birthday, the young king's council approached him and pleaded with him to take a new wife.

"Keep your beloved Gold Tree here, if you wish, but the nobles are talking. No one likes a mad king, and a new wife will appease the people."

The young king waved them away, obliging them. "Very well. Find me a new wife. I don't care who she is, for my heart will always belong to Gold Tree."

In a few days, beneath a summer moon, the young king married again. His second wife was wise in the ways of the land. She understood the medicines of the flowers and knew the best place to watch the sunset. She seemed ancient and young at once, this second wife, but as he had said, his heart belonged to Gold Tree.

The second wife was told of the king's first wife, of her beauty and the power in her voice. She knew she had died tragically, but she did not know that her body was still there in her house. Whenever the young king would go hunting, he would forbid his second wife to go into the room with the red door.

"Go anywhere you like, as always," he would say. "But leave the room with the red door be."

She listened for a while, but after they had been wed for nearly one year, she was determined to discover whatever secret the young king was hiding. She found the key to the forbidden room in the king's treasure box, and when he left for the first spring hunt, she went to the basement and unlocked the door.

She gasped. She didn't know what she had been expecting, but it surely was not to find Gold Tree, breathless but beautiful, still looking as she had looked in life, lying on the ground with a silver thorn in her finger. The second wife recognized the thorn as poison, pulled it from Gold Tree's finger, and the long-dead shining one took a great inhale. Her breath returned to her body, and she sat up, full of life and health.

The two women shared a moment of mutual compassion and empathy and, in only a few short days, became quite close. When the king returned from the hunt, he found his second wife smirking as if she had a secret.

Knowing the answer, the second wife asked: "Oh, my king, you always look so sad when you return home. What could I ever say to bring you joy?"

A lone tear ran down the young king's cheek, and he replied, "Oh, but ... if Gold Tree could live again."

Second wife grabbed the young king's hand and led him to the cellar. He protested, knowing what she might find there, but she pulled him along. He gasped, seeing the red door wide open, and then made a sound of astonished and joyful disbelief when he saw his beloved Gold Tree alive and shining. They embraced, and as they did, Gold Tree somehow knew, somehow remembered, the king's utter dedication to her, how he slept there at her side each night and still shared stories from his life. Her spirit had always hovered close, you see, for she knew she was not destined to die in this way.

The three of them, the young king, Gold Tree, and the second wife, were quite happy together as the days grew warmer, as Gold Tree's birthday approached. They planned to have a grand party, to show the kingdom how whole and well they all were, but as it had before, Gold Tree's birthday brought a terrible dream to Silver Tree. Again, she dreamt of her daughter, beaming with the light only she had ever truly had, and she woke full of worry.

In the mirror, she saw an aging queen whose silver bark skin had begun to flake and fall away. Though she knew her daughter to be dead, she went to the well, demanding the trout speak.

"One last time, little trout, I ask you: Who is the most shining one of all?"

The trout swam in a circle, shivered once, then answered: "Gold Tree."

Silver Tree pursed her lips and bit her tongue so hard it bled, poising for eruption. The trout swam to the bottom of the well to escape her ire, and she wailed and knocked every stone inside the well, sealing it for good.

"Gold Tree is dead. Gold Tree is dead," she repeated, running home in a mad fury. She was a living storm, this queen. She was a demon of destruction with a singular desire.

"Gold Tree is dead," she muttered, sailing south to her daughter's house, packing all the poison she could find.

At dawn on Gold Tree's birthday, she rose to sing at the sunrise, second wife at her side. The king had gone to find Gold Tree gifts and make the final arrangements for her birthday feast, so the two women were alone when they saw the early-morning light glinting off the silver bark skin.

"It's my mother," Gold Tree said. "She'll kill me for good this time; I know it. There's no way out."

Second wife saw Silver Tree differently and was not afraid. "Let's go meet your mother," she said.

At the dock, Silver Tree was coming toward them in the small boat, holding a chalice between two hands and smiling.

"Oh, my dear daughter. It's so wonderful to see you. Again, they told me you were dead, but … here you are! I've brought you a celebratory libation." She came ashore, holding the cup out for Gold Tree to take it. "The happiest of birthdays to you, my only child. May you have many, many more."

Second wife stepped in between Gold Tree and Silver Tree. "Queen, with all due respect, you are on our land here, and it is customary in this kingdom for the one who offers the drink to take the first sip."

Silver Tree seemed annoyed but pretended to oblige, holding the cup of toxin to her lips. In an instant, the second wife tipped the bottom of the chalice up, sending the liquid to run down her chin and into her nose and mouth. Silver Tree coughed and spit, falling to the ground and swiftly turning to an old, dead tree.

Together, the second wife and Gold Tree gathered the tarnished silver branches and buried them deep in secret places, covering their graves with heavy stones, that Silver Tree would never rise again, that Gold Tree would forever shine, and shine forever she did.

And so it is.

## 7.6. Whiskey and Forgiveness
### *Silver Tree's Eulogy*

Last night, my inner shining one held hands with my wisest self, and together, we put a predator in the ground. We made resin from rot and stacked stones on the grave, that she not rise again. We sang her soul home by remembering her in the days of her innocence, and we spilled a eulogy of whiskey and forgiveness from our cups. To you, my inner vampire who never wished me well, I say rest in a deeper peace in death than you ever knew in life.

## 7.7. The Hag Kept Singing
### *A Prayer-Vision for the Wounded Healer*

There is a steadfastness to the wounded healer's nature. They do not become easily pulled toward their wound, identifying only with the labels that name their injured nature, and neither can they be completely consumed by their healing journey. The wounded healer is our inner hag who keeps singing through our sorrow, joy, anger, ecstasy, and grief. The seas of human emotion rage on, but the hag keeps singing. This is her prayer.

Holding my grief like a slow-dying hatchling, I sought out the wisdom of the pipe-smoking hag. My plans were to prostrate myself at her feet and lament fallen queens, to bemoan the state of the world, to weep, to be soothed to sleep by the rhythm of her low-groaning rocking chair and be gifted some great maxim that would calm and cool all my boiling parts. When I found her at long last, she was singing a tune of oak and holly straight into the smoldering ashes of a neglected fire, an otherworldly owl perched on her shoulder.

The epic moment I envisioned failed to fruit, and the crone had no comfort for me. She scarcely looked up from the sizzle, unbothered by my particular tenderness, and I fell to my knees like a wounded babe, howling and kicking and beating my fists bloody on the ground. Thunder was rolling in the west, and I clawed my hands into the coals and smeared steaming ash on my cheeks. I sank my teeth into moss and spit dirt at the storm. On and on my tantrum dragged, the spell of the irrational, and the old one let me exhaust myself, her song uninterrupted by my fit, her owl unmoved, and her rhythm giving roots to my rawest rage.

My flesh softened around my bones in time. My blood chilled just a bit, and my wild shrieking quieted to feeble whimpers.

Still, the hag kept singing.

A lightning bolt ignited some primal flame beneath my ribs, and I roared a final, vicious poison hex at the lawmakers, at the arrogant beasts who claim rule over this boneyard land, scavenge and feed on fear, and wear crowns woven from lying tongues and family gold. I puffed my belly broad, gnashed my teeth, and retched that old guttural sound of a Witch threatened with the stake. My body twisted into an otherworldly shape, and I was a living curse. I was a death sigil. I was a wrathful banshee's torment and an eternal wail.

Still, the hag kept singing.

The rains came then, and the last of the heat hissed from the fire like the ghost of hope leaving a dying warrior's body. I collapsed into a heap of fragile flesh, and I let the waters wash the mud from my lips. I let the wind take the rebellion from my heart, and I wondered if it was the smaller stories I needed now. I wondered if I might put my most epic myths to bed and speak instead of the quiet under-tree ceremonies, of the solitary fireside rituals, of the secret hexing of systems, and of the late-spring storms. I wondered if the stories we need most offer us more than a war won, and still, the hag kept singing. I wondered what might happen if we stripped the shining armor from our flawed heroes, and the hag kept singing. What other worlds might we find if we slowed our pace, burned the map, snuffed our lanterns, and squinted into the shadows? And the hag kept singing. What songs might we learn if we pursed our lips and put our ears to bark?

And the hag kept singing, and singing, and singing.

## 7.8. The Underground Bone Cave
*For Women in Need of Reproductive Care*

When the monies are gifted and the petitions signed, when the word's been spread and the battle songs have been sung, I am left with little but a poet's ache. In those somber moments when my reach feels short, my vision is long. I can see for a million miles into the realms of deep time, where those underground bone caves are still tended by the skull-faced midwives.

They, these heathen queens who weave the cosmic tapestry from our many threads of fate, whisper prayers of protection for the wombs of the world, for the babes carrying babes and the women whose waters break in the fields, for those in need of courage to cross the battle lines drawn at clinics or leave the violent house, for the ones who weep behind locked doors in fear of a sky god's wrath and those who bleed in silence and solitude.

If you listen, you can hear them singing for you, these ancients before there were ancients. Alone in a story shared by billions, you cannot be. Held by the mystery behind all mysteries, you are. May those who fight a dead war on the autonomy of a body meet these skull-faced midwives in their dreams and be stung awake by their song, and may the medicine find its way swiftly to those who need care.

## 7.9. I, Chiron
*Prayer of the Mythic Wounded Healer*

The Greek mythology of Chiron illuminates the archetype of the wounded healer. He was a great medicine keeper who could not stop bleeding, yet he still shared his healer's wisdom. This is his prayer.

Some say the gods left these lands long ago, but I say the land is god. I, Chiron, say we are still here. Sing for us.

Tonight, I limp along this broken path with an aching belly and a medicine bag full of the poisoned arrows that took me down. Strangers on the road call me fringe dweller and turn away, but the old hooded hags who see me coming wink and gift me a traveling cake. A true healer must be wounded, these medicine women know, for only those who bleed know how to stitch a cut. Only those with broken bones understand the treasure of a splint and the necessity of a long convalescence.

Beware the healers who show no wounds, who claim to know no sorrow, who would kick my good leg and take me down. Beware the wounded ones who show no healing, who claim to know no joy. Both would sell you a snake oil brewed from their own bitterness. Neither will soothe your soul.

Some say the gods left these lands long ago, but I say the land is god. I, Chiron, say we are still here. Sing for us. Sing for me.

## 7.10. The Place of Birth, Blessing, and Death
*To Protect a Healing Space*

Here, birth will take a seat alongside death. The beauty of new beginnings will hold hands with what withers, and I will cast healing spells upon the hearts of those who seek my counsel. Grant me the wisdom to wield my medicine well and with great care. Let only those who will find the healing they seek enter this room where all stories are welcome. Should my medicine be harmful to any passing soul, let them walk past this door. This room is a temple, and my healer ancestors encircle this space from the north, east, south, and west. By root and branch, this room is blessed. And so it is.

### 7.11. A Good Story's Skin
*To Wish while Stitching a Wound*

A good story's skin is scathed by the unimaginable; by the sudden marks that surprise, delight, and disturb; by the punctures of the unexpected in our best-laid plans' perfect flesh. May this wound heal swiftly and well, leaving only the scar of a good story behind, a moment marked only in memory, a wild tale told at the fireside long after time has soothed and smoothed this skin.

### 7.12. Swift and Now
*To Bid a Breech Baby Turn*

Turn swift. Turn now. By our healers' breath, we call upon the loving spirits of the heathen midwives to come close and bid this baby turn. To the nameless grandmothers and the long-gone forebears who watch over this sleeping soul, we say come. Guide the babe's weight in the waters of the womb. The hour is late, and our prayer is of the most urgent kind. Turn swift. Turn now. Turn swift. Turn now.

### 7.13. Hawthorn Heart
*To Whisper When Healing Is Hard*

The candles are lit, and the spells are cast, but still the healing will not come. Some wicked mornings, when the glow of dawn stings my eye just right, I trust there is a molten gold core behind the prickly walls of my hawthorn heart. I know there is a treasure buried inside the muck of this wound, a hidden gift I will someday retrieve and tuck away in the archive library of my soul's cathedral, but for now, this healing is hard. May my wise and future self call me forward. May my nameless grandmothers lift me from this haunted sea, and may I remember to listen when the whispers of wild spirits find me in this underworld and call me their kin.

∽∾

# 8

# THE BOOK OF THE NAMELESS GRANDMOTHERS

*Prayers for Ancestral Healing,
Lineage Exploration, and Forgiveness*

*Somewhere, in a time long gone* that strangely still is, a circle of grandmothers holds council in a wooded grove. Their prayers are for their grandchildren's grandchildren to be whole and well, for the wounds of their lineages to be healed, one birth at a time. These hooded crones gather to name holy their bloodlines, to bid the living ones — their breathing ancestral altars — forgive themselves, to make art from the ache.

The crone archetype is a familiar one, but familiarity does not signal integration. The overculture has been organizing to silence the crone for centuries. The systems that dare to govern us were created without her input, and the Earth has been bleeding ever since. The prayers in The Book of the Nameless Grandmothers are for the inner hag to grandparent the inner child, for the parts of us who uphold the worst ills and isms to invite the shunned elder over for tea so they might teach us a thing or two about healing. These songs are the hymns of the wise one whose voice echoes behind our ribs, without whom none of us would be. These prayers are their prayers and yours.

## 8.1. Inside the Stone Circle
*A Prayer of Heathen Remembrance*

Some part of my heathen soul is eternally kneeling inside a circle of standing stones, whispering prayers in a language I cannot speak, singing to stars I cannot name, and falling in love with a world I might call small that ends at the sea's edge. This quiet echo of who I once was lives her whole life there between the monoliths, and if nothing else, I am her living dream.

## 8.2. Stores of Salt and Honey
*An Anthem for the Resilient Daughters*

A long winter wants some salt stored on the shelves, and the granddaughters of resilient women know the merit of a stocked root cellar. There, we keep cans full of skills we dare not speak of, ready to open when the hour demands. A jar full of spit and hellfire here, sealed up and soaking in vinegar. A brandy-and-mugwort tincture of healing stories there, ready to open when an old wound begins to bleed. May we clean the dust from the lids now and toss out the spoiled syrups and over-sugared jellies. Bitterness keeps longer, they say, but resilient daughters know salt and honey are good forever. Preservation and sweet medicine never spoil; may we keep both in our secret stock as the lights grow dim.

## 8.3. Remembered Magick
*For the Grandmothers Whose Names Were Stolen*

Some memories and medicines live inside our bones. A teacher may help us remember, orienting us toward a lost knowing, but the wisdom was already ours, sunk in the marrow by our foremothers, woven into the double-helix spirals of our ancestral inheritance.

Your name is lost, but your magick lives in the marrow. I know not how to find your grave, my heathen grandmother, but your recipes, prayers, and poetry are buried in my bones. Tonight, I am your shrine. I cast this spell for me, for you, and for the children who will speak such prayers to me long after my flesh has become food, long after these words are covered in moss.

## 8.4. The Cast-Iron Cookpot
*For a Grandmother Gone to the Grave*

A better human I am to have known you, my matriarch-in-spirit. I shall keep your memory in a cast-iron cookpot that forever bubbles inside that hag's hut in my mind. Visit me often, Grandmother. Find me in my dreams and bid me become wise. Find me in my waking hours when the to-do list is long and sing me a song of blackbirds, broken cradles, and treetops. Remind me to keep my innocence even when madness lurks in the shadows. Remind me who I am, the grandchild of a great woman who spoke the old language. To you, today, I say thank you. I shall keep your memory well.

## 8.5. My Grandmother's Garden
*To Name a Lineage Whole*

When the longing to belong is great, we find sanctuary in those small memories, those times when a place claimed us as its own. This is a personal prayer in memory of my grandmother's peculiar garden. May you find medicine here, too.

When the recipes have faded, and the old language is but a broken echo half heard in the caves of my dreaming time, I conjure a medicinal memory of my grandmother's garden. Full of scallions, potatoes, and harsh lessons, it was. Tended well and with great care when those twin beasts called progress and development only lurked on the fringes of her wilds, my grandmother's garden was a humble thing to behold. In the eastern corner, a doll's head balanced unevenly on a twisted sycamore branch, our makeshift scarecrow, dismembered innocence intended to terrify, our horror-story garden guardian.

In the summer, the doll's head housed a wasp nest, and my young self wondered what it might be like to set the stinging monsters free.

In my mind, they were trapped there under pink plastic and glass eyes, caged and unwittingly enrolled in the garden's security system. Now, as time has taken both the garden and my grandmother to their graves, I know the wasps chose to be just there, and somewhere in the intricate web of cosmic memory, my soul chose to be there, too.

Comforted by this knowing, I am. Swaddled warm within the strange wholeness of the beyond-human story, I find myself on these dark days of war and wildfires. Our lineages are not broken but frayed and reknotted to form to a stronger lace. Our ancestral altars are built from aching memories, old wounds packed with salt and ash, and small gardens full of gratitude. May we tend them well.

## 8.6. Brewed by Memory and Muse
### *A Song for a Lonely Night*

This night when loneliness is my unwanted guest, I hear the wisdom of these times in the slow-rolling thunder. I scry my prophecies of heart healing in the flame of my low-burning oil lamp, and I dance with the reaping bone-woman when she visits to say, "You are surrounded by your most beloved dead, by your nameless grandmothers and wild angels. Never are you alone. Never are you without one hundred thousand spectral hands at your back. We are here."

## 8.7. The Little Match Girl
### *A Bedtime Prayer-Story*

Some stories show us the darker shadows of the psyche, promising no happy ending to our human struggle for wholeness. Collected by Hans Christian Andersen, "The Little Match Girl" is one of those tales, a story of grief, innocence, injustice, and ancestral wounding that, like every life, ends in death. There's a reason this story finds only strange homes in popular culture. Even so, this tale is hardly without its vital lessons, for it illuminates the despair that emerges when the soul's desires misalign with society's demands, the undue burdens placed on the innocents by modernity, and the medicinal kinship inherent within the mother line.

This is a teaching tale for the innocent visionary, the one whose world does not match their dreams, and the nameless grandmothers who walk as ghosts beside them. Let this story illuminate what needs to be seen. Allow every character to reflect a part of you; you are the innocent and the stranger, the weeping father and the knowing hag. As with all stories and all dreams, look for the questions that nip at you after the story ends. What would having the answers to these questions mean for you, and what shifts might occur from gathering these missing pieces?

Once in a time that came and went and is now here again, there lived, breathed, and danced an innocent. This innocent, this girl child whose heart had known little grief, lived in a land new to industry. In a humble town full of soot and chimney smoke, the innocent reveled in her regular journeys to the woodlands surrounding the village.

When the days were warm, these near-daily excursions with her mother and grandmother were full of learning and love. The elder matriarch taught the young one where to gather the best firewood, how to harvest the root vegetables, and when to call a fruit ripe or rotten. The child's mother showed her where to find the clearest mountain spring and how to carry water home in winter without breaking any bones.

Though the land provided for the small family well, they could not pay their rent in berries and mushrooms, and the father, much like the rest of the men from the village, forsook the land-tending ways of his own father for work in the factories. No one spoke about it, but a certain grief took up residence in the hearts of this town's men, hearts that longed for hands in the dirt and open fields but instead found themselves beating in time with factory whistles and the metal-on-metal clanking of commerce.

The women held on to the old ways as long as they could, but in time, even they succumbed to a modern amnesia. The innocent's mother and grandmother were among the last to sing the old songs, the last to remember that vital dance between the fallow and the fertile. The child had learned much in her few short years, and she was quite happy in her youth, having known little fear or loss. Alas, as it always happens, death came to her house.

One winter when the innocent was but ten years old, her grandmother fell ill. The forest had no medicine for her, and the local doctor would only accept money as payment; they had none, and the old woman was dead before the Quickening Moon dawned. The passing of the elder matriarch broke the innocent's mother's heart in two pieces, and by the following winter, she, too, was ailing. For weeks in the deepest of snows, the innocent had to go to the forest alone, struggling to remember all she had been taught about where the winter cabbages grow and brewing homemade medicines from the dried yarrow her grandmother foraged before her death. The little one's love was not enough to save her mother, and before the spring rains could wash away the last of the dirty ice on the streets, she took her last breath.

The small grief fissure that had opened in the father's heart, the wound that began bleeding from doing daily work that starved his soul, widened all the more now. Without his woman, without his land, he woke weeping, finding joy only at day's end when he took sanctuary in a bottle of whiskey and drank himself to sleep by the fire. By midsummer, the father was working only to pay their rent and buy his drink. What little food they had was gathered by the little girl every day, but it was scarcely enough to sustain them even when the forest was lush with life.

As autumn drew closer, the little girl was afraid. She didn't remember enough. She hadn't learned all she needed to from her mother line, and now it was far too late. She remembered how to skin a rabbit but not how to salt the meat for the colder months. She remembered to can the parsnips and the wild strawberries but not how to keep the air out of the jars. By the dawn of October's Blood Moon, they had nearly gone through all the food the little girl had set aside for a long winter.

One haunted night, All Hallows' Eve, the little girl dreamt of her grandmother. Quite clearly, her grandmother told her there was a place nested deep in the forest, a place she had never visited because the walk was too long for a child, a place where hundreds of apple trees bloomed and fruited quite late in the season. "Go tomorrow," said the grandmother in the little girl's dream. "Go tomorrow at sunup and carry as many baskets as you can. Follow the stream east for half a day, and you'll find this bountiful place. Collect all the apples you can, can them well, and you will just make it through the coldest months."

The girl woke while it was still dark with a fire in her heart. For the first time in a long while, she felt full of purpose. She stoked the dying fire, covered her father with a blanket, and set out carrying every bag and basket she could find. Remembering her grandmother's words, she headed east toward the tree line, walking with such determination she almost didn't see the man in the top hat who stood at the forest's edge.

"My, my, my," the stranger said. "Where are you off to in such a hurry?"

The little girl could see the stranger more clearly now, the sun rising behind him. He was standing with one foot on top of a massive, garish trunk. She had been taught to be wary of strangers, so she nodded once and continued on, walking right past him toward the sun.

"Wait, girl," the stranger called after her. "I won't bite."

She was half running now.

"How would you like to make some money?"

She slowed her pace a bit, feeling safely distant from him, though she despised that word. She didn't really understand money. She knew there never seemed to be enough of it, no matter how long her father's days were. She knew it didn't grow in the forest, and she knew its absence was the reason her mother and grandmother were gone. She turned around and faced him.

"What if I told you that inside this trunk was the answer to all your problems?" he asked, tipping his hat. She edged closer to him, holding curiosity and caution in equal parts. "Do you want to see inside?"

She narrowed her eyes at him but nodded.

"Wonderful!" He clapped his hands once and knelt to open the trunk. She stopped, keeping a safe distance. "Don't be shy," he said. "Come. Have a look."

She took a deep breath, and in that moment, she could swear she smelled the wild rose oil her grandmother wore, and she froze.

"No," she said, taking a step back. "I have to be going."

"Aww, it will only take a moment," said the stranger. "Hear my proposal. If you don't like it, you won't have wasted more than a minute of this glorious day. Come!"

She sighed, took three steps toward him, and lifted her chin to peer over the edge of the trunk. It seemed to be brimming with small white boxes, hundreds — no, thousands — of them.

"Matches?" she asked, brows furrowed.

The stranger clicked his tongue. "Not just any matches, my girl. No, no, no! These are the finest matches ever made. Hand-dipped by yours truly. There are ten thousand matchboxes in this trunk. You can sell them for a penny. It's nearly winter, and everyone needs their fire."

"I can sell them?" The little girl was confused.

"You sure can. All I want is half a penny for every box you sell. You keep the other half. Sell all these matches, and you'll have fifty dollars."

She swallowed, knowing well that fifty dollars was more money than anyone in her house ever had to their name. Fifty dollars would have her and her father eating like kings through the winter and planting an abundant garden come spring. Fifty dollars would put a smile on her father's face, a great treasure she had sorely missed.

As it always happens in the old stories when a bargain is about to be struck, cities rose and fell in that decisive moment. The birds stopped singing. The wolves stopped roving, and the eyes of the world were on the innocent.

"All right," she agreed. "You have a deal." With that, the stranger shook her hand and walked away, leaving her and the trunk at the forest's edge. She looked east and thought about hiding the trunk under some branches and returning for it after her journey but considered that if the stranger's promise held true, she wouldn't need to waste the day walking and gathering apples at all. In the end, she left her baskets there and spent the next few hours dragging the trunk home.

That night, she stood outside the pub frequented by her father and most of the other factory workers in town. She asked everyone who entered, most of whom she knew by name, if they would like to buy some matches to light their winter fires. By night's end, she had sold nearly thirty matchbooks. The wheel of fortune had truly turned in her favor, she thought. What she didn't realize was that most of her sales were because of pity; all her customers knew she had lost her mother and grandmother. They further knew her father was at the pub more than he was home, and they spared what change they could to make the little girl smile.

Pity has its limits, of course, and by the following week, the little girl was only selling one or two matchbooks each night. People in the town were poor; they knew to keep a lit fire burning and, furthermore, knew how to start one in the first place. Matches were a luxury, an indulgence few could rationalize on the cusp of winter. By December's new moon, the little match girl had gone a week without selling any matches at all. She had 9,950 matchbooks left and was without any prospect of selling any more. What was worse, she was sure the apple grove her grandmother spoke of in her dream was barren by now.

Desperate and without much hope, the little girl sat in front of the hearth, lighting scraps of wood with her matches that would burn for just a few minutes before becoming ash. Her father was humming and slurring himself to sleep, and the little girl decided there was no better plan but to go into the woods and find that grove. The snows had not been too terrible yet, she thought. Surely, there would be a few apples left on the ground.

Into the night she went, pulling her threadbare coat close around her. The baskets she had left there by the forest's edge were gone, but she told herself she could carry the fruit in her skirts if she had to. It was near midnight, and she remembered her grandmother's directions. The stream was frozen, but she could follow it. The wolves were howling, but she felt she was somehow protected by some unseen ancestral force. If she kept going, she should find the grove at daybreak. In her mind's eye, she held the vision of herself happening upon a vast stretch of trees, the garnet-red fruit glistening with frost in the morning light; this vision kept her warm for a time, but soon the cold began to claim her.

No longer could she feel her feet and hands. The snows were much deeper here, but she had gone too far to turn back home. She stuffed her hands farther into her pockets and felt something there she had nearly forgotten. She still had the matches in her coat she'd been hoping to sell the night before. Stopping beneath a knotty elm tree, she dug a small hole in the snow and filled it with the few thin twigs and dead leaves she could gather. Striking the first match, she struggled to light the frost-coated leaves. The twigs, too, were frozen, and the fire wouldn't light. Again and again, she tried, burning through an entire matchbook in less than a minute.

She wanted to cry, but the cold wouldn't let the tears come. Her hands shaking, she pulled another matchbook from her coat and whispered, "Grandmother, help me. I need a fire." The match blazed to life, glowing with an otherworldly amber light that illuminated the snow and ice, casting a sudden spell of warmth upon the whole forest. In that gold glitter-scape, the little girl saw the most exquisite vision.

Where the pines, elms, and oaks once stood, there was an abundant banquet table, brimming with the innocent's favorite foods. She could almost smell the fresh bread and meat pies. Her mouth watered, and she reached out her hand to touch a shiny red apple. As she did, the flame from the match was snuffed by a brisk wind, and the magickal banquet table was gone. As the vision disappeared, so did the warmth the little one felt. She was shaking again but managed to light another match.

This time, she saw a vast room glamorously decorated for Yule. A tree as tall as any that stood in the forest loomed large in the little girl's vision, decked with silver garlands, candle cups, cranberries, and ginger cookies. Beneath the tree were lavishly wrapped gifts, and the little girl was again warm all over. "Let me stay here," she whispered, but as soon as the words left her lips, the match went out. All was dark.

Again, she struck another match, hoping the beautiful tree and gifts would reappear, but this time, instead, she saw her grandmother. Rosy cheeked and full of life, her grandmother looked as she did when the small family was happy, fed, and well. The little girl reached out to hug the elder she had missed so dearly, but the match was flickering out. Quickly, she lit another to keep her grandmother's spirit there. Her grandmother seemed to be speaking to her, but she couldn't understand what she was saying. Again and again, she lit another match, and each time, the grandmother's voice became clearer.

"Let's go, my child," the grandmother was saying. The little girl could hear her clearly now, and together, they walked through the forest. No longer cold and shaking, the little girl was so incredibly happy to have her grandmother with her. She hadn't felt safe in so long. Her spirit had been so vexed with worry these last long months, the sort of life-and-death worry not meant to plague an innocent so young, but with every footfall in the snow, she felt her fear dropping away like dead leaves from a branch.

"Don't leave me again, Grandmother," the little girl said.

"Oh, you needn't worry about that, dear girl," the grandmother said. "We're nearly there."

In what seemed like only seconds, they arrived in the bountiful apple grove, and it was suddenly like late summer here, with the fruit trees blooming in all their glory. The sun was shining, and the little girl danced in the warm wind. Her mother was there, too, joyful and well, and together, the three wild spirits sang a song of renewal, nourishment, and peace.

The next morning, a band of hunters found the little girl, frozen solid and surrounded by dozens of burned matches. The town wept for her, their little match girl, lamenting the dreary state of their world, the times that would allow such tragedy, but the little girl's spirit was whole and full of wonder, made so by both gratitude and grief.

And so it is.

## 8.8. If Only
*Lament of the Little Match Girl*

My pockets are full of possibilities, this night when the ice is a thick prison for my hope. If only I had more kindling. My mind is full of fruitful memories, this wicked midnight when the wolves are howling. If only I had help to harvest these buried-by-time wisdoms. If only I could be visited by a knowing hag who knows me better than I know myself, who can help me sort this from that and prepare for the uncertain days ahead. I call on the wizened foremothers now. I'm sunk in the snow and need a paper-skinned hand to lift me from my melancholy, to bite me to life once more. Lost in feckless fantasy, I am, and I must remember how to build a good fire and keep it hot. Come close, Grandmother. In this endless winter, come close.

## 8.9. Come Closer
*To Bid the Way-Back-Still-Here Ones Join Us*

We must be wary of locking the ancestors in a prison called the past. They are still here, with our loving ancestors resourcing us, giving shape to our perception, and entering into our awareness whenever we choose to look.

Join us, this night when the stars blink in a rhythm more joyful than our beating hearts can find. To those way-back-still-here ones who still sit around the ancient fires and speak of bone-women, fetches, and green dwellers, we say come closer. Remind us of our heathen home.

### 8.10. By Moon and Sea
*A Song for Traveling to Ancestral Lands*

So long have I been homesick for a place that lives in my blood but not my memory. I go there now, to this place where stories live in the moss, mud, sands, and rainwaters. I go there now to recover an unnamable piece of my wholeness. May I find what I seek, by moon and by sea.

### 8.11. By Your Hands
*A Healing Spell for the Grandmothers' Lost Arts*

The time of snow and shadow was upon us, and the jubilant hag who sits atop my ribs and skips stones in my blood made new demands. Leave nothing undone, she said. Harvest what's hearty now. Gather your people. Stack the wood high. Take your lessons from the mountain dwellers. Stock salt. Build a better fire.

I raised my hood and did all she asked of me, her aging house of flesh and bone. I walked against the wind and collected the fallen apples, shriveled rose hips, and dried twigs. I readied the well. I sharpened the axe. These were the days of the pitiful sun, and that old crone sang a weaver's work song while my skin went dry, while a pale sun rose behind the gold-and-garnet trees.

The land was still and ready under a sky swollen with storm. My mind was softening into a dreamscape full of ghosts, graves, bog bodies, and galloping corpses. I peeled the apples slow like Grandma Grace, and I prayed to Brighid like Grandma Mary. While my sweet brew bubbled, I heard a blessing from both dead-and-gone grannies, and the winter-rich hag who tugs on my tongue joined them in their Pagan prophecy:

*May you meet these dire times well, dear daughter. May the remedy for your apathy be awe. May you stand on the northern hill, ring a bell, look west, and hum while the sun sets on your tamer ways, while the crumbling binaries burn and the new innocents quiver and hatch, while the impossible becomes possible and the clocks fall from the walls. Stay tender through it all. Stay wise. Walk with one foot in the world of the wailing women and the rebel chieftains who dreamt you alive.*

*Take the low roads to higher ground. Forget fate. Remember emergence. Teach your babes to be wonder-rich and fear-poor. Hone your night vision and look for the lessons in the old stories of devils, shadows, sunsets, and blackthorn trees. You know more than you think you know.*

*Keep watch over the stores. Line the sills with ash and salt. Lick the bottom of the jar. Waste nothing, not one drop of syrup or one daylit hour. Beware those who would sell you solutions, simplicity, or secrets. Bemoan those who draw hard lines between sovereignty and empathy. Befriend everyone else. The lone wolf dies on the longest nights no matter the length of its fangs or the thickness of its fur.*

*Stay warm. Bring the old ones in the woods soup and vinegar. Keep drumming.*

*You are the knowing crow and the clueless fawn. You are the angry kings you hate and the careless princesses you envy. You are hope and despair wrapped in skin and boiling apples as the veil grows thinner between light and shadow, right and wrong, living and dead, ancient and future. Stock your accounts with the new-old currencies of joy and jam, gratitude and grain, humor and honey, song and seed.*

*Name neighbors family. Name truth treasure. Stitch the holes, drop the hems, mend the coats. Keep laughing.*

## 8.12. The Sweeter Moments
*When the Mother Wound's Ache Is Great*

I remember your face, on these days when the hole in our shared ancestral story is a mouth I crawl into to keep warm. There, I name the sweeter moments treasure, and I leave the bitter and bleeding times for another day. If nothing else, my flesh formed inside a nest you built just for me. My small bones brewed slowly for ten moons, tended by our grandmothers' ghosts inside your womb cauldron until the time was just right for me to meet the light. So many years later, I am still here; for this, Mother, I say thank you.

## 8.13. The Cailleach's Supper
*A Meal Blessing on the Cusp of Wintertide*

The hours of light grow short, but our memories are long. To that old hag of winter who walks the rough and wild lands, who begins her journey as the sun sets on our autumn dreams, we say thank you. This is our Cailleach's supper, our annual initiation into the dark and deep. We eat this meal as if it were our last, as if our tongues might turn to ice at midnight. Here, we sip our medicine from our shared story and warm ourselves at the fire of kinship. Not a taste will we waste. Should we live to see the first snowfall, we will surely find sanctuary in the memory of this moment, a strange solace in a meal shared on the cusp of winter. And so it is.

∽∾

# 9

# THE BOOK OF THE PAGAN WARRIORESS

*Prayers for Battle, Bone Gathering, and Beauty*

*There are many different forms of war.* There are the battles fought for freedom from oppressors with blades and bullets and orchestrated attacks performed by million-dollar weapons. There are the sudden wars that erupt overnight at the whim of a mad king and the centuries-long conflicts that wax and wane. There are the old wars waged over imaginary land boundaries and the emergent wars between art and artificial intelligence, hopeful children and climate deniers, so-called liberals and conservatives. While we may think there is no worse word in our language, the etymology of *war* is derived from the old German for "to confuse." Whatever its form, a war perplexes the psyche, confuses our best judgment, challenges our morality, and, if we choose, inspires us toward honing our greatest gifts.

Our inner warrioress is tasked with preparation, with training, with a conscious and continual honing of the soul's innate skill. She is attuned to the alignment that exists between her inborn talents, the treasure of her genius, and what she is willing to fight for. Where she is gifted, she also finds a battle scar.

So easily could she join the old wars that ended during childhood; she knows just where and how they're fought, after all, and there is an odd comfort in continuing the long fight. If a war is meant "to confuse," then the old wars are far too familiar to befuddle us in the ways that inspire growth. There are those who condemn all war and instead declare peace on all parts of their lives, but in the end, they have embattled bits, too, as we all do.

The prayers in The Book of the Pagan Warrioress are prayers to protect the inner and outer innocents, soulful songs that sweep through the house of our memory and remind us of our victories and defeats. The inner warrioress honors the times when rage is righteous and so wisely chooses the battles that initiate change and bleed us into transformation. These are her prayers and yours.

## 9.1. Dreams of Witch Warriors
*When Rage Is Righteous*

Deep inside my darkest dreaming time, the Witch warriors have painted their faces with ash and moon blood. Their spears are spells, but their greatest weapons are called *memory*, *voice*, and *vision*. Fools never see them coming, but the knowing ones can hear their battle songs rattling the underground. Their plans are measured in generations, and their memories are long. Tonight, I pray these wildlings be Earth's bodyguards and creep into the collective imaginings of those who might just save us. In my wickedest nightmares, they hide under the boardroom tables of big oil and spit rivers of sand into the gears of this broken machine. In my greatest prayer dreams, the berserker poets and warrior dreamers take to the streets and sweep ritual mayhem through every golden door. Our Earth is a hunted Witch, but tonight while I sleep, the predators become prey.

## 9.2. See Our Joy
*To Giggle-Spit at the False Prophets*

Tonight, I am a hooded pyromancer scrying an oracular death song for the false prophets in the fires of my ire. Tonight, the first line of this dirge is this: *See our joy.* See our joy and be on your way, preacher. We repent nothing, and you can't sell our own belonging back to us. We'll find our own redemption in the forest and take our communion from the mountain stream, thank you very much. Watch, if you like, but our wild joy dances on, with or without a witness. Peddle your fear elsewhere. No one is buying your salvation here, so see our joy and be gone.

## 9.3. When the War Was Great
### *A Prayer for Disquieted Father Spirits*

Sent to war before your world was whole, you were. The youthful dreams of adventure, passion, and play replaced by the politicians' plans, and you, you poor boys, left to stitch up the bleeding wounds long after the battles ended, long after the medals were framed and your innocence died without ceremony. The great inner war began once the outer war was over, and your disquieted ghosts still haunt these halls. Rest now, I say. Your war is over. Tonight, I sing your soul home to the thin lands where the old ones will soothe your ailing spirit. No more need you hold these horrors. Let them go. Let them go. Let them go. Rest now. You are whole, and you are well.

## 9.4. You Will Live Well
### *For the Wars of the Father Line*

Our history books are war stories. The plotlines repeat. I write this prayer-poem as the daughter of a Vietnam veteran, the granddaughter of a World War II veteran, and the great-granddaughter of a veteran from both world wars, all drafted, decorated, and wounded in battle. May my sons write a new story.

Praying to a Pagan god inside a foreign land's prison is the spirit-echo of a criminal I might call great-grandfather. Caught between two world wars, he was. May he be visited at midnight inside his cell by a softly singing shadow he might call great-granddaughter. May he hear me when I say a hopeful poet will share his blood, and may he dream of a tender face that looks like mine.

Praying to the god of his childhood inside a snow-and-mud foxhole is the spirit-echo of a decorated soldier I might call grandfather. On the edge of an endless war, he was. May he be visited in that moment just before the shrapnel took him down by the mist-made ghost he will someday call granddaughter. May he hear me when I say, *You will live and live well.* May he witness a vision of sun and summer there in the underground of his soul's coldest winter, and may his heart beat slow, that the blood stay in his veins.

Praying to no god at all inside a jungle full of storm is the spirit-echo of a fallen warrior I might call father. Sent to fight in a fools' war, he was. May he be visited in that pregnant moment before the bullet cracked his helmet by a dancing soul he will someday call daughter. May he hear me when I say he will live a long life full of glory and good crime, and may he see the faces of his women reflected in the wild bark of a mangrove tree.

## 9.5. When War Came for Our Fathers
### *A Once-and-Future Prayer*

When small battles come, I remember I am the living ancestral altar. I remember black candles still burn there for the many wars fought by the fathers, for the fallen children whose small hands iced over in the snow gripping gun barrels, for the mothers left home weeping and the old ones who survived an age of bombs and bullets only to see another. Tonight, I send this Pagan prayer to the old gods of peace whose names we no longer remember: May a new story be written, and may I live to hear its once-upon-a-time.

## 9.6. Wolf–Mother Fangs
### *A Prayer-Song for the Warrior Mothers*

This is my spoken spell of venerating her-story, of honoring the nameless warriors who receive no medals for their heroic feats of motherhood, for the breasts bitten by babes and long hours lost to a tireless and unpaid work, for the restless days wet with sour milk and the dreamless nights drenched in sorrowful lullabies, for the endless battles fought with soulless insurance companies over a child's care with wolf-mother fangs as weapons, for the tears spilled on changing tables and NICU isolates, and for those rare quiet moments spent sobbing on cold tile and crying out for rest in a villageless world. To the mothers, we say thank you for your service.

## 9.7. The Impossible Possible
### *A Modern Song for the Steadfast Heroine*

When we are confounded by the complexity of these times, the confidence of others can seem suspect. We side-eye their certainty, and sometimes our skepticism is warranted. There are moments, however, when we might choose a conscious admiration of others' surety, allowing their clear vision, even a vision we do not share, to be an invitation. In these moments, this is our prayer.

Your boldness beguiles me, my fork-tongued friend. Your strength inspires me, and your certainty in these times always stuns me into silence. I want to question your ferocity; after all, how can one be so sure in these times of upheaval? The gods are rolling the dice with our fate, yet you stay steadfast and sharp-toothed. Just for today, I'm calling your conviction my medicine. I'm seeing that defiant underwater flame called hope alive in your eyes, and I'm naming you, the impossible warrioress, my timely muse. Thank you, you doubtless wonder. I am proud to call you friend.

## 9.8. The Witches' Justice
### *To Protect the Witch Warriors*

They walk among us, the Witch warriors fools never see. They are hexing big oil in their basements and putting the predators' hearts in bottles. They are whispering their weapons in midnight circles and dancing their battle plans beneath the redwoods. May they be well protected, these secret agents of the Holy Wild. May the way-back-still-here ones shield them with spectral hands raised in a time before time, and may they win the war against those who pillage the planet and leave the children shivering in the streets. To the secret sorcerers, we say we are you. Let us gather and uphold the Witches' justice.

## 9.9. Bluebeard and the Seventh Mad Maiden
*A Prayer-Story for the Fight*

When shadow men haunt the pages of a story or the wilds of our dreams, they might be tricksters or teachers, or they might be true villains. Bluebeard, in most interpretations of this story, is the latter. Bluebeard is the toxic predator, the stone-cold killer who knows neither guilt nor shame, but deeper exploration might reveal how our innocence is hunted both from within and without. To save themselves, sometimes the hunted innocent becomes warrior. This French folk tale holds a wealth of shadow lessons about the "bleeding keys" we hold to our own hidden darkness, about the secrets we keep locked away until the fateful time comes to bring them to light. It is in these moments when our innocent becomes warrior, when we open a red underground door to a long-buried truth and suddenly find ourselves ignited by purpose.

As you read this story, look to its sharp edges. What lessons lie there on the pricking points? What is revealed in the maiden's solitary moments, and where does your inner warrior find themselves inside this plot now?

Once upon a late-autumn moon, an innocent maiden was vexed by nightmares. By day, she gathered the last of the apples, laughed with her older sisters, and sipped spiced drinks by the fire. By night, she was plagued by vicious dreams of endless hallways haunted by screaming banshee women and headless corpses calling her name. To look at her by the light of day was to see a young woman of modest wealth enjoying her youthful years at her family's estate, protected by her status and envied by her friends. To see her at the devil's hour was to see a terrified creature skittering about her room and lighting every candle she could to keep the demons at bay.

As it always happens, though, the sleepless nights took their toll on the maiden, and by the last full moon of autumn, she was seeing shadows and hearing the howls long before moonrise. Those boundaries she had been told she could rely on between dreamscapes and reality, night and day, shadow and light, madness and sanity, became blurred as the days grew shorter and shorter still.

Her reason was compromised, you see. Her sisters and brothers began to worry for her, and her mother was in search of quick solutions. By great luck, or so it seemed, a solution presented itself.

No one remembers precisely how the rumors of the man with the sky-blue beard came to the manor house, but soon all who lived there were whispering the name Bluebeard, calling him a monster whose wives always went missing. Some people said he'd been married six times. Some said hundreds of women had gone missing from his house.

"He's on the hunt for a new woman now," the horse master said to the land keeper.

"Best hide the daughters," the land keeper said to the mage.

"There are things that cannot be undone," said the mage to the fire. "It's already been set in motion, this story. We must let it play out."

As it happened, Bluebeard was a wealthy trader indeed. His riches were such that his invitation to join him in the forest at the crossroads for a feast was difficult to refuse, or so the maiden's mother said, and all the daughters were ordered to wear their finest gowns. The brothers insisted on coming along, having heard the terrible whispers about this beast with a blue beard, and the older sisters were quite skeptical.

"I'm not even going to speak to him," said the oldest sister. "I don't care what Mother says."

"Last night I dreamt his blue beard was full of snakes," said another, but the youngest sister, weary from her nightmares, had little fight or conviction left inside her. She no longer knew who she was or what she wanted in life, and this is a dangerous state to be in around predators, is it not?

The forest feast was a true banquet in the wild. They say there were fifty tables overflowing with a bounty of fruit, pie, meat, and wine for only ten guests, and they say everyone gave Bluebeard a wide berth except for the mother and the youngest sister.

"Come, my lord," said the mother, seeming quite taken with Blue-beard's charms. "I want to introduce you to my youngest daughter. Forgive her, as she does not know the ways of the world as yet. She has seen very little outside of our manor's walls."

The brothers and older sisters watched the encounter with nar-rowed eyes. They watched their mother lead the monster to their sister. They watched while the mother left her alone with him, and they watched in horror while he gave her a goblet of heavy wine and proceeded to be very, very friendly with her, the poor innocent. As the hours passed and the fires began to die, Bluebeard and the maiden danced and laughed.

"He was so charming," the maiden said to her sisters as they rode back to the manor in their carriage. "You should have given him a chance. His stories! His eyes! I've never met anyone quite like him."

"You listen to me, sister," said the oldest maiden. "You cannot see him again. If he sends for you, refuse. If he gives you gifts, return them. If he promises to make all your dreams come true, don't dare believe his lies. It will be the death of you."

"Hush!" snarled the mother. "Do not envy your sister's happiness just because you have yet to marry at your age. Bluebeard is a good match."

"All his wives have gone missing, Mother," protested one of the brothers. "You are selling our sister to the devil!"

"Nonsense! You've no proof. Unmarried men are always targets for gossip, and gossip is for the weak-minded. Your sister needs to marry. She's not well, and to be a wife is to have a purpose," spit the mother. Nothing more was said that night about Bluebeard, but the maiden's dreams were more terrible than ever. She woke the whole house with her screaming, and the next morning she heard her mother whispering outside her bedchamber.

"A proposal just one day after he met her! What great fortune! She can hardly refuse. Have you seen the circles under her eyes? The man's more saint than devil that he wants to marry her in the state she is in."

The maiden, in her weakened way, believed her mother. How could such a charming man be a monster? What if this was her only chance to marry? Before the first new moon of winter, they were married, and the maiden was overwhelmed by the grandeur in which her new husband lived. She had never seen so much gold in her life. It would take her lifetimes to explore the whole of the grounds, she thought. But the excitement was short-lived.

The first days of their marriage saw the maiden become even more ill. She began nodding off over meals and hearing those voices of the screaming women at all times. Bluebeard did not seem worried about his new wife in the slightest. He also did not seem to be in a rush to consummate their union.

"Dear wife, I can see you're in a state. Surely, the wedding was taxing and you miss your people. I'm going away for a few weeks on business, and I'd like to invite your family over for a wonderful Yule celebration. I've already sent for them."

The maiden's heart quickened because, yes, yes, this was exactly what she wanted, to see her sisters and brothers.

"Here are my keys," said Bluebeard. "You may go wherever you like. My home is yours. Walk the gardens. In the kitchen you will find anything in the world you'd like to eat. Be well, and when I return, we shall live together as husband and wife from now until forever."

The maiden was delighted, bubbling over with gratitude. She threw her arms around her husband in thanks and for the first time caught a whiff of his beard; it smelled of blood, and there was no mistaking it, that reek of iron and salt.

She felt imaginary hands grab her and pull her back, and a shock — a visceral, creaturely repulsion — went straight through her like lightning. She was a fawn who embraced a wolf. She gasped, but Bluebeard did not seem to notice.

"Oh, the smallest key," he added. "Don't use that one."

The maiden saw it immediately, a tiny silver key with the smallest skull engraved at its head.

"All the other keys are yours to use as you please, but do not dare use the smallest key. Do you understand?"

She rolled her fingers around it with an intrigue she could not name, and the spectral women who screamed in her ear grew loud.

"But why —" she started, and he roared at her then, grabbing her throat with one hand and looming over her like a demon of the night.

"Do you understand?" he snapped.

She nodded, swallowing, shaking.

"Good," he said, composing himself, smoothing his coat and waving farewell. "I shall return in one moon's time."

The maiden spent the next week in a dreamlike state, wandering the long hallways carrying her husband's keys. She could feel eyes on her always. She was never alone, though the immense house was presumably empty. She dreaded the nights and could hear women crying and screaming from behind every door as soon as the sun dipped below the horizon.

Her family never arrived.

She missed her sisters. She missed her home. Broken, she was, but she didn't know by what. She had no name for this madness that overtook her, and without anyone to keep watch, she became more ghost than girl.

It was not until her thirteenth night alone that she began going from room to room, unlocking every door and leaving them wide open. Most of the rooms were full of books, massive pieces of furniture draped in white cloth, and black trunks full of jewels and fur. Some rooms were empty except for a single painting of a woman on the wall. Each time she approached a new room, she'd hear a woman scream from behind the door.

Sometimes the voice would just wail with terror, and other times the voice would order her to stop, to leave, or to run. She started to scream back before she turned the key, and it became a strange ritual that somehow brought her comfort, a peculiar ceremony for her peculiar mind.

By sunrise, she had unlocked almost every door. Her fingers were bleeding, and her throat was hoarse. She couldn't remember what it was to sleep.

An unexpected sound — laughter? — came from the kitchen, and she followed the noise to find the room full of her family. All her sisters and brothers were there, and she dropped the keys on the stone floor she was so startled.

"Are — are you really here?" she asked timidly. "I didn't hear you come in at all. Were you here all night?"

Her sisters started giggling and singing a love song while her brothers began building a fire.

"Of course we're really here!" her oldest sister said. "We were worried about you. How is your beast of a husband?" She led her to sit near the hearth.

"He's — he's away."

One of her other sisters picked up the keys from the floor. "What are these?"

"He said I could open every door but one," the maiden said faintly. Another sister brought her something hot and steaming to drink. "I've opened them all ... but one."

Her sister held up the smallest key. "Well, what are you waiting for?"

"Oh no. I mustn't."

"How will he know?" Her oldest brother puffed up his chest. "We'll lock it up straightaway. Ole Bluebeard will be none the wiser."

The maiden shook her head, but her sisters and brothers were already walking down the stairs into the dark root cellar.

"Where are you going?" the maiden called after them, lighting a candle and following their voices.

"Come on! Hurry!" they beckoned, but the screaming women were louder than ever. The maiden lifted her shoulders up toward her ears, but the terrible sounds were so loud. When they finally quieted, she was alone, standing in front of a red door. The tiny key was in the lock, unturned.

"Where — where have you gone?" She scoured the dark cellar for her family, but there was no one there. She called every name, searched every shadowy corner, but there was nothing there but her and the red door.

She edged closer to the door. It smelled like blood, like Bluebeard had smelled before he left. The air was thick with it, and her stomach lurched.

"Are you in there?" she asked so quietly her voice was almost a whisper. "Sisters? Brothers?" She knocked lightly just once, then three times. The silence was deafening. It had not been this quiet inside her head in so long. She almost felt she could curl up on the dirt floor and go to sleep.

"I — I'm going to open the door now," she said to no one, suddenly certain her family had never been there at all. Her hand shook as she turned the key, and she heard dozens of voices weeping and wailing, "Noooo!"

But it was too late. The door creaked open, and the terror of her nightmares did not compare to the sheer, red, raw horror that lay before her here. The room was immense, the floor so wet with blood that it poured onto her feet when she opened the door. The stone walls ran garnet red, and it reeked of rotten flesh. Skinless, cracked skulls with long hair still sprouting thin from the ivory floated in the blood. Headless bodies at varying levels of decay hung from the walls, and her lone candle lit it all in a spectral glow.

Time stopped. A single drop of blood from above fell and snuffed her candle, and the breathless maiden slammed the door and turned the key, feeling her way back up the stairs and to the kitchen.

Her heart was a speed drum. She tasted bile. The hem of her nightgown was stained red, and she stripped herself bare in the kitchen and burned it. She felt a drop of blood in her hair and severed both her braids with a butcher's knife, throwing them to the flames.

The keys seemed clean except for a small drop of blood on the tiniest key, so small you could barely see it, but the maiden knew Bluebeard would surely see the evidence of her betrayal. She scrubbed and scoured the thing. She boiled it for hours. Still, the drop of blood remained. She wept and she scrubbed, wept and scrubbed, until the sun began to go down yet again.

She would not stay here, she knew. She had to get out. She had to leave before Bluebeard returned. She left the soiled keys in the kitchen and ran through the ice-covered garden toward home. It had been months since she slept for more than an hour, and there was little she could be sure of anymore.

What was becoming of her?

She used to know so much for sure. She used to have hope. Now, here she was, running through the winter woodland naked as a deer, without even her hair, leaving behind all promise of a normal life. The image of the tiny bloodstained key was burned in her mind, consuming her even now, as the snow started to fall. She began to lose her way in the storm. Her feet were as blue as her husband's beard, and she was swallowed by a fatigue so great she could not escape it, curling her body into the snow beneath a massive pine tree. Strangely warm, she began to drift to sleep. Slowly, surely, the maiden sank below that deep dark river of consciousness.

There was beauty, heat, and bliss here. There were no screams, only the faint sound of wind and laughter. She thought she caught a glimpse of her grandmother, but she was too far away. The snow was falling here, too, but the flakes felt warm when they touched her skin. This was the heaven she'd been looking for her whole life, she thought.

"Do you wish to stay?" a voice asked, and she turned to see dozens of women behind her; she recognized some of them from her dreams, but here they were, whole and sound. There was no blood, no scars, no weeping. "You can stay here with us. You're very safe here."

"Am — am I dead?" the maiden asked.

"Not yet," said one of the women.

"I don't want to die," the maiden said truthfully. She didn't. Of course she didn't want to die.

"We didn't want to die, either," twin voices spoke in unison. "But we knew too much."

"Do I know too much?" the maiden asked, but she knew the answer. "It's lovely here, but I don't think I'll stay. Not yet."

The women looked at each other, sharing knowing glances and murmurs.

Suddenly growing very cold, the maiden shuddered as the faces faded. The wind grew louder, and all the beauty and bliss was gone.

"Let's get you home," a low voice murmured, and she had the sensation of being lifted from the ground. She heard horse hooves, and she smelled blood and snow.

The next sensation she was aware of was the sound of a crackling fire and a man humming. Fear gripped her. She was returned to Bluebeard's house, and here he was. Had he found his keys? Had he seen the blood? She pretended to stay asleep, but it was no use.

She could feel the heat of his breath as he leaned over her, and she prayed to every god she'd ever heard of to save her.

"You're very lucky, girl," Bluebeard said. "Had I not decided to return early from my travels, you would have frozen to death last night."

She held her breath, finding herself fully clothed and covered in blankets so heavy she could barely move.

"Tell me, what sent you running like that?"

Something in his voice told her that he knew. The mage told her once that a man could never be evil and foolish at once, and this man they called Bluebeard was most certainly evil. Maybe he'd been born so, or maybe the world had marked him in such a way that he could never grow whole; it mattered not. A beast he was, and innocence was his prey.

She peered over the blanket just enough to see the blue of his beard in the firelight, and the silver keys on the table. The keys were sitting in a red pool, as if they were bleeding. She looked for a weapon and saw nothing. She was in the kitchen, so close to the root cellar and its room of horrors. Something about her hopeless circumstances made her bold, and she sat up.

"Why have you no servants here?" she demanded to know.

He looked straight at her with curiosity but said nothing.

"No one would stay in such a place."

He laughed. "There are those who can stomach such things quite well. Not an innocent like you, of course, but there are those who are drawn to the darkness. I am not alone in my proclivities."

She thought about bargaining with him and decided against it.

"You never sent for my family," she accused, and he smiled.

"No," he affirmed.

She sighed. "So how is it to be, then? You bring me to the bloody room and cut off my head?"

He stood and walked toward the fire, moving the wood with a poker. "If your luck continues, yes. Do you think you deserve an easy death?"

She heard a faint sound in the distance then, but she couldn't quite place it.

"I did like you," he muttered. "At least madness is interesting. The other wives were so boring I could scarcely wait until they used the key. I wanted to kill them at the altar."

She thought about how many more women would die after her, and the sound grew louder. Bluebeard did not seem to hear them, but the maiden was sure they were horses. Had her family come for her after all?

The sound grew louder, but Bluebeard kept talking. "I remember all their names, you know. I remember their faces."

The maiden stood, legs shaking. The horses stopped, and she heard shouting. Her family was here! Bluebeard kept staring at the fire. Why didn't he hear them? In an instant, she grabbed the butcher's knife she'd used to cut her hair, just as her brothers and sisters appeared in the kitchen.

Her sisters gasped at the sight of her. Her brothers' weapons were drawn, but they stayed back.

"Do it!" they said, and she took three steps toward Bluebeard and slit his throat from ear to ear.

The blood flowed, turning his beard violet, and he reached for her, feebly. She saw the silver key bleeding rivers onto the ground, and soon the kitchen floor was covered in blood. Still more of the red stuff started pouring in gushes from the root cellar, and with the blood came the bones.

Her family was suddenly gone again, and she was alone in a flooding manor house, her dead monster of a husband gasping for his last breath. Surrounded by the ghosts of every woman he had ever killed, the maiden dragged the helpless Bluebeard into the garden, walking into the winter and leaving the drowning house behind forever. They say the vultures and the raptors came for him then, picking him apart and carrying his pieces to the far corners of the world.

And so it was.

### 9.10. Behind the Red Door
*For the Darkest Pieces*

Such horror I see here, as I hold the bleeding key. The red door is open, and inside that death room I see the bones of every woman I once was. I see the slaughters of the heathen daughters. I see the blood rivers of my ancestral darkness carrying the broken skulls of the innocents, and I cannot look away. This is the most brutal room I keep in my house of memory, and here, I know how beastly the inner monster becomes when we lock him away. Tonight, he roams freely and leaves blue hair and bloody footprints on the snow. Tomorrow, I shall name myself warrioress and call him home. For now, I'll wait while the blood pools around my ankles and holds me in place just here, at the threshold beyond which my darkest pieces lie.

## 9.11. The Lost Women
*To Speak When the Witch-Hunters Knock*

This evening sky is an altar to our enduring sovereignty. The stars will not be eclipsed forever by the shadows of dark robes and stone pillars, nor will we. These older-than-ancient mountains will not be governed by the rule of a crumbling order, nor will we. May our rising fire tide of voices incinerate the Witch-hunters' judgments. May our howls blow the ashes of unjust laws to the winds, their dusty remnants carried to the grief sea by reckoning rivers of long-dammed-never-forgotten ancestral memory. May we be marked by this cracked-by-crisis moment and remember we are sovereign even now, even as we sing our songs in the streets from an aching dusk to a haunted dawn thick with our grandmothers' ghosts.

## 9.12. A Home Remembered
*When Comfort Comes Slowly*

Those who identify closely with the warrioress archetype find a peculiar sanctuary inside the fight; they breathe easier on the battleground than they do in the soft nest of their beds. When whatever old war they were fighting ends, they continue to stand their ground against no one but their own ghosts. Times of peace seem misaligned with their purpose, and they reenact battles as if the old war is their only home. When the voice of the deep soul comes creeping to remind them of their worth beyond any weapons they may possess, to deliver the message that the war is over, it hums low and soft under the tired echo of the war drums' beat. In these moments, this is the warrioress's prayer.

Comfort comes slowly after a day when rest was rare. The heart-drum's cadence refuses a steadier rhythm, and the breath knows no ease. Here, by my will, I bid a soft memory rise from a deep place and be medicine. I take solace there, in that warless home remembered. I remember this moment has a living spirit, and even now, this fleeting crisscross of time and space, my most potent elixir, is still breathing with me. May my own pulse slow-dance with this memory's breath, finding a gentler pace, and may I return to the here and now restored.

## 9.13. The Tear-and-Bone Gratitude Altar
*To Remember before Sleep*

Most especially when the day's been hard, I build an altar of gratitude in my mind before sleep swallows me. Here, I place a bone for every small thankful moment I lived from dawn to dreaming. I choose to remember the spaces between the battles, those quiet moments of nondoing to-morrow's memory might miss, and I leave a tear for the fleeting breaths when sorrow hugged at my heart, remembering that grief is born of the wildest gratitude. May I sleep well, this night. And so it is.

∽✜∾

# 10

# THE BOOK OF THE BOTANICAL BABE

*Prayers for Innocents, Beginnings, and Wild Children*

*To be innocent is to not only see* the infinite possibilities of existence but to refuse to name them, to see the world as if we are always blinking awake. The innocent holds the tension of an infinite morning, keeping a quiet hope alive even as the tribulations of a treacherous world loom. Some might say the innocent's eyes are narrowed by naivete, but to look through the eyes of an innocent is to see as a small god sees, naming everything a seed that houses an impenetrable vastness; to this end, the innocent is the wisest among us.

.The uncertainty of these times beckons us all toward innocence. We cannot know exactly where climate collapse, the advent of art made by artificial intelligence, or threats of nuclear war will lead humanity, and both innocence and arrogance are a choice. To choose innocence does not mean denying wisdom sourced from invaluable experiences gathered over a lifetime. Conscious innocence means acknowledging that sometimes we have no map to follow, no pattern for these moments we are living. Reason will only get us so far, lost in these wilds, and sooner rather than later, we will need to take our rest on a rock and consider radical action.

The innocent is a pattern breaker. Anyone who has had an earnest conversation with a child has met the power of innocence. They ask a question that nips at your knowing and changes the shape of your understanding forever. They shock you awake with their wonder and invite you to reanimate your curiosity, leaving you with no choice but to become a little wilder for having met them in their play, in their unscripted drama of child meets world.

The prayers in The Book of the Botanical Babe are the prayers of the innocent, songs sung by seeds as they stretch toward the sun for the first time. Imagine your inner innocent blinking awake on a forest floor, suddenly born again at dawn with eyes thirsty for every shade of green and ears perking at every creaturely sound. These prayers are their prayers and yours.

## 10.1. Morning Song of the Orphaned Dreamer
*To Speak upon Waking*

This morning of all mornings, an innocent babe is finding herself alive in a new way. I remember her face from my darkened dreamscape, and I can see her wide eyes now even as I blink away a sleep tormented by to-dos, should-haves, and must-bes. She, this knowing fawn, bids me wake as a child wakes, with a numinous hope that all will be well, full of a heathen faith that this day holds just one mystical moment that is my most profound and timely gift. May this moment be mine; I will seek it out, and I will listen to that dream child now as the dawn gives birth to possibilities I cannot yet name.

I will rise well and parent my orphaned dreams, tending to my inner knowing hag who understands the nature of these times, reminding myself I am under contract with my own heathen truth: that I chose to be born here and now for a reason my soul keeps secret, and that I will live better this day for having met that wild child in my haunted dreaming time. Just for today, I see the world through the eyes of a small god. Just for today, my vision is illuminated by the light of ten thousand infant stars, and I, the wizened child of wonder, know what it means to dream the world awake.

Here, may the peculiar brilliance of this new day mark my feeling flesh with soul-scripted sigils only the mountain wolves can read. May they howl-sing a heathen benediction for the miracles I will surely be met with on this day, calling these scripted moments forth from the caverns of deep time, gifting the wilds of my waking dreamscapes with an otherworldly richness my older-than-ancient self remembers. On this, the dawn of all dawns, I see what I must see. I know what I must know. I am who I must be, so into the dewy woodlands I go.

I'm marking an initiatory moment, this day of generative befuddlement. Taking a radical respite from my binding dualities, I am. May I see beyond those narrow passageways named *this* and *that*. With every footfall, may I become full of faith in that strange and misty third road, choosing emergence over any presumed destiny. I'm writing the poetry of this moment in spit on stone, and I'm dreaming of futures far wilder than even the freaks could ever imagine.

## 10.2. Incantation for Thirsty Roots
*To Sing into the Ground*

Into the ground, I sing. I lick the earth and taste the truths buried there by my foremothers. I give breath to their memories, and I bless this forbidden garden with spontaneous hymns rising from my inner altar. To these seeking roots below my feet, I howl for you now. Reach long and wild into these fecund depths where you were born and still belong. Be mothered by the mud. Be fed and full. You search, as I search, for the satiating nourishment of untamed ground, for irrevocable belonging, for your own fullness of purpose. To you and your exquisite becoming, I sing, I sing, I sing.

## 10.3. A Graveside Birth Song
*To Mark a Coming Rebirth*

Just before this dawn and every dawn, I am a lone child kneeling before a headstone and humming a dirge for who I once was but am no longer. Death wants the dark. So long have I carried the bones of who I used to be on my back. So long have I been shrouded in a cloak of dead skin, but I leave my old selves here in this graveyard now. I leave them here, and

I stack stones as a grief ritual for the weighted masks I no longer wear. For my too-timid voice, I place a stone. For my shamed maiden and shaking child, I sing, and I place a stone. To the small and weeping one who still fears the night, to the careful maker who tucks their art away in the dark never to be witnessed, to the lustful poetess who hides the skin of her soul under a shroud of worldly judgments, I say rest in the deepest peace. Here, I stay while the cairn rises with the sun.

## 10.4. Protection Prayer for the Motherless Fawn
### *To Keep a Wild Child Safe*

When you leave, my wild kin, I carry a hologram of your splendid heart inside the hollow of my belly. I bid my fiercest ancestors thrum their scythes on the ground and walk with you through the haunted night-scapes of this world. May you see them when your inner fires hiss under the icy rains of foolish betrayals, remembering you are shielded by the snarls of one hundred million wolf-mothers. May you hold the heat of this one knowing in your hands: never am I far.

## 10.5. Birth at Sunset
### *To Welcome the Wild Unseen*

The inner innocent takes notice of the Otherworld, allowing the visions that would confound the rational, experienced mind to become teacher, holding the tension of the strange without fear, seeing every omen as if for the first time, noticing the way the weather participates in their experience, and softening their gaze enough to sense what is hidden behind the material. In these moments, this is the innocents' prayer.

Though the hours run swift these days of rising seas and wildfire, I trust the gloaming will gift me a strange and otherworldly vision to slow the rhythm of my anxious heart-drum. At sunset, I will look west, ring a bell, and welcome the wild unseen. May my many ghosts haunt me well, carrying away my modern regrets in their ancient hands, and may I be reborn beneath an amber-violet sky. To the new day that dawns only at dusk, I say thank you.

## 10.6. A Spell for the Seeds
### *To Enchant a Garden*

A garden wants a dedicant, and today, that green-blooded disciple is me. As this god star we call sun casts its ancient spell upon this soil, I join the choir of my Earth-loving grandmothers in their timeless song of quickening and joy. Steward these roots well, my dirt-keeping ancestors. Learn the songs of the elementals and sprites who already call this ground home. May the storied bones buried beneath these blooms add their own poetry to your soulful, heathen hymns, and may this garden I am blessed to call mine for a time sing-speak its own rebel songs through me, a Witch of the wilds.

## 10.7. A Hymn for the Nameless Hatchling
### *To Bring Clarity to a Wish*

I hold a small-boned wish in my hands like a mewling hatchling. Try as I might, I just can't dream this holy want awake. For all my feverish desire, this quivering creature refuses to grow, but if I listen close to the honey-tongued poetry of my inner wise one, I remember my secret sight. The old hedge-dwelling hag who tends the thorn-and-bramble garden inside my ribs says, "See." See not with the dim glow of a lone lantern but with the brilliance of a many-sunned morning. See now. See better. See now. See best.

Lick away the afterbirth. Cradle this newborn close. Call it whole and well. Build an altar nest for this bleary-eyed babe and nourish it with stories of your trials and triumphs. Tend it with small gifts of song. A neglected wish is a shadow, and shadows left imprisoned become our most cunning monsters. Keep the sun shining on this dream you hold dear, and a rainbow-feathered beauty it shall be. Come nightfall, watch with the attention and pride of a mother hawk while this wish spreads its wings and flies moonward.

### 10.8. Blessing the Beating Heart
*To Protect a Pregnancy*

I wished for you when my dreams were small, and though the wilds of my world have blossomed all around me in flowering vines of art, sorrow, and tenderness, I wish for you still. I bid my fiercest forebears who knew the ways of birth come close to me now and chant a heathen song in an ancient tongue. They, these holy midwives, shall stand around my bed while I sleep and bless this babe who calls my body home with every incantation they know. In a quiet gesture given them by the old gods, they will enchant my womb with a gold-and-garnet light only you can see, my already-beloved innocent. Be warm. Be well. So soon shall we meet. Until then, know you are my most treasured vision. Meet me in my dreams and share your secret name with me.

### 10.9. Gathering the Treasure
*To Pray while Foraging*

This day was spilling its bounty into my most luxurious dreamscapes last night, and now I understand the meaning of treasure. To this land, I say thank you. These strawberries are the rarest rubies. These blueberries, the most precious sapphires. In my Pagan queen's throne room are hanging garlands of emeralds called nettle, mugwort, and mullein. At my cookfire, I shall slow-brew a cauldron full of liquid riches made from those beauteous amethysts called elderberries. And if I be so blessed, this basket full of gold and garnet will become medicinal pear and apple sauce, sugared to perfection and stored for a long winter. To the spirits of this most majestic place, I offer you a gift bundle woven from poetry, hair, and gratitude. To this soil, I offer you my eternal devotion and a vow to tend you well and forever. And so it is.

### 10.10. Maturity's Lockbox
*To Bless the Playful Hours*

I keep a lockbox tucked away in my mind for days such as these. For a few long hours, I shall contain my maturity here, lest my to-do lists, calendars, and screens keep me from my wilder ways. Should an errant thought arise that reminds me of my obligations, I'll send it swiftly to its room. This is a day of play, I say. These are the goalless hours when curiosity is king, and I'm naming my inner innocent my most experienced wilderness guide. A child I am today, and I hereby bless this day of play with a wink and a giggle. On to the forbidden ground of preposterous mayhem I go!

## 10.11. Welcoming the Wildling
### *To Bless a Birth*

Anyone who doubts the divinity of life has never beheld a birth. To witness flesh born from flesh is to truly know the timeless waltz between birth and death, the eruption of screaming life from those twin bloodied thighs of yesterday and tomorrow. Today, I bless this birth. May the loving ancestors whisper soothing songs of protection, grace, and understanding into the babe's heart, guiding the innocent through the dark caverns of becoming and gifting them to the light. May the Fates hear this soft song and seed this new life with love, art, and belonging. May the once-upon-a-time of this glorious story be consecrated by great health and great joy, by tearful smiles, womb water, and tenderness. And so it is.

## 10.12. Crossing the Threshold
### *To Mark a Rite of Passage*

A true rite of passage demands the traveler come face-to-face with their own death. Monsters guard the threshold of rebirth, always. The dying one's spirit must be witnessed here, in all its fleshless splendor, as it crawls toward death's door. It must be seen by both the loving ancestors and the vicious beasts who say "Go back now or we'll kill you." Facing death means facing birth, and crossing the threshold means burning the return journey's map.

Into the woods, I went. I knew nothing, only that I must go. I carried nothing, only a traveling cake baked by long-gone-still-here ancestors.

Witnessed by dragons and wolves, I was. Eaten by the great mouth of despair, my bones were picked clean by the raptors, licked dry by the forked tongue of loneliness and left there at death's threshold. I scarcely recall my red slow-drumming soul crawling out of the birth canal, but here I am, breathing again for the first time. To my ancestors, I say name me. I am no longer the one who boldly marched into those wilds. Name me, and mark my rite of passage with a song, story, and celebration.

### 10.13. The Fool's Pathless Path
*To Bless a Heathen Pilgrimage of Spirit*

If a life is, in part, a spiritual quest, it begins by finding roads paved by others. Swami Vivekananda said, "It is good to be born in a church, but it is bad to die in a church." Heathens might disagree with the first assertion, of course, but the statement can be applied to life areas well beyond religion. We learn the rules so we can find their vulnerable places and break them. We find a container in which to learn, a lens that narrows our worlds enough so we can best hone our vision. When the time is right, when we've gathered all the medicine we can digest, we leave the small house built by someone else's hand and venture into the wilds. We cease to walk the mapped path that many others have walked, and we find the pathless path where no other feet have tread.

Today, I set out on the pathless path. I name the unknown my most treasured teacher, and I honor all who have walked this unblazed trail, all who have left these wilds just as they are — overgrown, unmanicured, and without a name. When the sunlit hours stretch long into the haunted gloaming time, the silver-lipped sorceress called moon will show me the meaning of fate, exodus, and homecoming. Lost in the pulse of eternal time I will be as I light a lone candle on the road, singing the last lines of that oracular song of journeying and hill walking. Dancing in the delight of complete and irrational joy, I will be. Wait for me.

# 11

# THE BOOK OF THE SHEPHERD
*Prayers for Nurturing, Self-Love, and Space Tending*

*Deep within the spring meadows* of our heathen minds there
lives a part of us who has become the caregiver we needed when we
were younger. They are our inner nurturer, a cunning shepherd to the
chaotic flock of wounds and wants we have all acquired over a life lived
well. Their voice is a soft one, hushed under the louder voices of our
inner dreamers and fearful protectors, but if we listen, their prayers are
for our wholeness, for care of the soul and a felt, embodied connection
to the creaturely world.

Imagine the prayers in this, The Book of the Shepherd, spoken and
sung by a heathen shepherdess who tends her flock in solitude. She
is alone but not alone, encircled by those who care for her in return,
who wish for her to tend to herself as she tends to them. These are her
prayers and yours.

## 11.1. Beside a Haunted Meadow Hearth
### To Bless a Solitary Evening

Here I sit beside a meadow hearth most haunted. Tonight, my ghosts
are memories of mages and mountain dwellers, fabled characters I have

met along the way of my storied life. I bless this solitary evening with pyromancy and soft songs, and I welcome the visions that come.

## 11.2. Singing Over the Butter
*To Name a Meal Medicine*

This meal seems ordinary, but the bread's been blessed by a healer's hands. The butter's been sung over with heathen hymns to stitch any broken heart, to gift swift hope to any who despair, to bring a joyful dream vision to any tongue silenced by sorrow. The wine's been consecrated by this Witch to inspire oracular conversations of strange imaginings, and the greens have been graced by incantations of innocence and wisdom. This medicinal meal is my most nourishing spell. Bite by delectable bite, may all who taste these wild flavors be oriented closer to their soul's truth. May they find a home here at my table, nested beside a guardian spirit who sees the splendor of their worth. And so it is.

## 11.3. Honey Tea and Peppered Poetry
*To Send to a Heartbroken Friend*

For you, my friend, I've prepared a meal of honey tea and lightly peppered poetry. It's not much, I know, but I hope it serves you well now, when it's the simple medicine that matters. Sip for sweetness and listen for spice: heartbreak tenderizes the soul and opens us to the next possibilities in life. Just for today, let an indulgent memory find you and swaddle you in woolen nostalgia. I love you, this day and every day. Should you need a foulmouthed and fair-minded friend, I'm yours. I'll cook you dinner and tell dirty jokes while I do it. I'll walk with you beside the river and bid the current carry away your strife, and I'll sit with you by the hearth in silence, willing a new story be born from the fire. Until then, I am here. And so it is.

## 11.4. The Apocalypse Table
*To Share with Fellow Freaks and Wildlings*

In these divisive times when every local, national, and global happening invites an immediate battle, when many have forgotten how to speak to those who do not see the world as they do, the freaks need each other. Those of us who understand we can be different kinds of people and still share a garden, who can look each other in the eye and listen without agreeing, and who know the worth of our shared humanity need each other. This is our prayer.

Come sit, my friends. My apocalypse table is set and ready. Tonight, I've prepared a feast of soup and story, of apple-buttered bread and laughter. Only my most beloved freaks are invited, so, please, if you will, take a seat and tell me what you love. Let's leave nothing out. Tell me of your fear and your envies, your joy and your sorrow. Let's lament our orphaned dreams and lay them to rest. Let's scry our future in a slice of pie and weep at the kinship we've missed. Not a breath will we waste here, as our songs get loud. Not a tear will fall unnoticed. Today, we remember why we chose to visit this wild place called Earth, and we hold each other's hands in an undying devotion to creaturely indulgence, to gathering, and to giving. Today, we remember the beauty of found family, and we are full of faith in the human spirit, in our beyond-human belonging. To you, my most precious freaks and beloved deviants, I say welcome. My table is your table.

## 11.5. Melting the Bullets
*An Altar-Side Prayer When Innocence Is Lost*

To be hopeful in these times does not mean to close our eyes to the worst atrocities, to the ongoing madness that sends children to their graves. We know both hope and prayer are insufficient protectors, but prayers are a sound and necessary supplement to our petitions and protests, to our votes and our voice.

On this, a most fitful evening, the moon is spilling celestial dirges into the mythic garden where innocence is tended. We go to this ground to weep, to name holy the children of light whose brilliant soul fires burn on with a heat that can melt any bullet. We go to the garden to bid a better dawn bring healing to the spirits who ache for the small eyes that closed too soon, to the hearts split open by the gravest of tragedies. On this, the evening of grief, we weep for innocence lost, we plant seeds of hope deep in the soil for a more just world to bloom bright, and we cast a spell to enchant action well beyond thoughts and prayers.

### 11.6. The Moss-Walled Palace of My Mind
*To Whisper on a Solitary Walk*

Every step is a step away from my ache and into the moss-walled palace of my mind. With each footfall, I come closer to a bolder way of being in this, the beyond-human age of emergence. Here, I see the precise truths I must see in a gilded mirror. Here, I find a lost reflection of my own belonging, a long-gone-still-here memory of my most ancient blueprint, my heathen origin story locked away in the light. With every step, I see more clearly. I see, I see, I see.

### 11.7. These Vast Pastures
*A Prayer-Song for Protecting the Flock*

We left these fields open by choice, but on this wicked evening when the wild hunt roams, we call forth those vigilant shepherd spirits from the four directions. Come now, you strong and steadfast keepers of the old ways. Stand in the north, raise your arms, and become wolf to keep the beasts at bay. In the east, spread your wings and screech out a raptor's song. Uncoil, rise, and unfurl your serpentine hood from the south. In the west, be sea beast and shape-shifter, for you hold the secrets of the waters, wells, and seas. Protect my wild flock on this, the night of all nights. Encircle these vast pastures and keep their peace. Calm their hearts and tend their spirits that I may rest well this night.

### 11.8. Return, Return, Return
*To Bid a Lost Creature Come Home*

My home is full of an aching absence tonight, and I bid the wild and ghostly shepherds keep my beloved safe. Guide them well. Bring them home. Keep watch while they walk, and hold a lantern only they can see. Tend their fear and open their ears to my mourning song. *Return,*

*return, return!* I say. Your bowl is full, and your wild mother longs to clean your fur and hold you close. Come home, sweet babe. You've left a hole in my house, and I'll rest curled there in the void until you make your way back to this nest.

### 11.9. In the Goat's Eye
*A Healing Salve for the Caregivers*

An old hag shepherdess wanders these woods and whispers, "Some follow their bliss, but caregivers follow their calling." In a goat's eye, the tired healers scry their visions on the edge of sleep, where they listen to the work songs of the Pagan medicine keepers. May they rest well here. May they receive that rare reward of sensing purpose fulfilled and soul restored, and may they see great beauty in that goat's eye, great gratitude born of every soul who still lives because they live. And so it is.

### 11.10. Ancestors of Lion and Wolf
*When a Beloved Pet Dies*

So deeply have I cared for you, my most beloved creature. You watched me weep when hope was lost and my human friends were few, and tonight these twin rivers of tears flow in your memory. May your wild ancestors come to carry your soul swiftly into the Otherworld, where you shall surely wander free, with the vigor of youth, the beauty of a lion, and the wisdom of an elder wolf. Someday, this Witch will join you there in the lush lands of spirit, but for now, rest and roam at your will. Visit me in my dreams and show me your joy. I love you.

### 11.11. Call of the Mourning Doves
*A Dawn Song When Self-Care Is Needed*

The beauteous beast called sun is rising once more, but I am still carrying a lantern through the dark of night. Even now, as the dawn is a cosmic egg cracking open across the violet sky, I carry a dim light through a wild graveyard where all my old selves lie buried. I pour song, whiskey, and crumbled peat over the cracked and crumbling stones that bear the worn names and dead dreams. I wear a dreamer's veil hand-stitched by my most forgiving ghosts, and I hear the call of the mourning doves waking me to a day of care. I will tend to myself this day, I swear. I will sip slowly and bid the hours take their time. I leave my worries here in the boneyard, where the spirits will keep them caged, and I set my mind toward renewal.

## 11.12. Prairie Skirts and Open Pastures
### *To Bless a Land Left Wild*

For a time, I find myself home here in these untamed fields where the grasses are long and the winds blow swift. Somewhere, a piece of paper bears the name of some modern owner, but today, this paper means nothing to either this land or me. Today, I wear a prairie skirt and carry a picnic basket full of salt, bread, and blessing herbs. I bid this land be forever protected from the human storm, and I leave an offering of story here, in return: Once upon a time, a land and its many spirits were left wild, and they lived happily ever after. The end.

## 11.13. Beauty in the Rot
### *A Prayer for the Swamplands*

Tonight, my dreams are carved from soft peat and rough bogwood, and I'm finding beauty in the rot. I welcome the wisdom of the creatures that slither below these dark waters, and I revel in the inglorious stink of compost as my old self dies. These swamplands are where I'll leave the last of my old names, shed like snakeskin and left on a sacred stone for a death-eating raptor to find and feast.

∽∾

# 12

## THE BOOK OF SHAPE-SHIFTERS

*Prayers for Time Weavers, Human Evolution,
and Strange Futures*

*A shape-shifter moves into a form* that lives closer to what they love. Tales of shape-shifters orient us toward that forbidden place where our humanity meets the uncivilized nature, where our modernity meets a wild animal in the woods. There is a part of us that longs to become creaturely, to return to a world some part of our soul remembers, despite its lawlessness and hidden dangers.

If we dare to trace the many forms we have taken over our life journey, we might easily name ourselves shape-shifter. Our wise and future self is always calling us forward, enticing us toward our greater form, and we know the shape we find ourselves in now will not be our last. Above all else, the shape-shifter prays for truth, and they hold tight to their wild pelts that remind them who they are when the false skin falls away.

The prayers in The Book of the Shape-Shifters are prayers to befriend our less civilized nature, not to overly romanticize a life without convenience or the blessings of modern science but to keep true to what it means to be this beast called human. We are here to be a creative animal, and should we find ourselves in a cage that keeps our purpose from the world, we shape-shift and slither between the bars. In a long life, we do this over and over again, shape-shifting into forms that feel true then truer still, that won't be caught by the trappers. We hide our wild pelts in secret caves, and we find our kin in communities of fellow freaks. The shape-shifter prays for their untamed nature to be protected, because it is there, in that strange and secret place, where their greatest art is seeded.

Imagine these prayers spoken by a seal-woman lounging on a salt-stained rock. In her human form, she holds her slick black pelt in her hands and dreams of both land and sea, both rootedness and freedom. These are her prayers and yours.

## 12.1. The Otherworldly Creature on the Road
### *To Bless a Journey*

While the inner warrioress might disagree, the shape-shifter understands we are cocreated by the people and places we encounter. We see our worlds differently when we visit a new place. We behave in new and wild ways when we are removed from our everyday schedules or speak to a stranger whose words sting us in just the right places.

Sometimes, our inner shape-shifter requires a good journey, a pilgrimage of the uncivilized spirit that can reset our modern minds. The journey might be a small one. We need not cross any seas or climb any mountains. We need only open ourselves to meeting the otherworldly creatures on the roads, those who do not think quite like we do, who can somehow illuminate exactly what we need to see, exactly who we need to become in order to move closer to what we love.

On this, a most heathen midnight, I am setting out on an unknown road to a nameless place I'm calling tomorrow. I'm packing a traveling cake and a gift for the otherworldly creature I shall surely meet at the crossroads. Be it a cunning fox or a one-eyed raven, I will offer that seer-trickster a sweet treat and a gold coin, bidding my travels be blessed by the wild unseen. On this, the night of all nights, I am rich beyond measure. My pockets are full of possibilities, and I'm well on my way to becoming my wisest self. When the dawn finds me, I shall surely be in a better place. For now, I welcome the journey that comes. May I tend the road well, befriending the dance between what was and what will be, taking my direction from the invisible spirit of my soon-to-be self.

## 12.2. Autumn's House
*To Sing into the Ashes*

Both autumn and spring are the shape-shifter's seasons. These are the seasons of changing winds when both birth and death are afoot, and the shape-shifter is at home here. The changing seasons are invitations to both manifest and banish, to be midwife and death doula. In these times, this is the shape-shifter's prayer.

My autumn house has a soul now, as the medicine of sacred solitude calls me into the woodlands. Long ago in a lost time, my soul painted a secret sigil on the door to remind me what wildness really means, to bid me leave my modern, rotting fears on the porch for the wolves to find and feast. In the hearth, I'll build a fire and name it my kin. When the winds blow from the west, I'll watch from the window while the leaves break from their branches and dance. When loneliness comes creeping, I'll take solace in this timeless sanctuary where nothing and everything is revealed, and I'll sing into the ashes of the dying embers when the first snows begin to fall.

## 12.3. Keep Wild
*To Tell the Children*

Your world is full of storm, sweet child, but the skies and seas have seen such things before. The old Witches know a crisis is a door to possibilities. Disintegration births renewal. Dawn follows the dark, so keep wild, child. Something splendid is afoot. May your eyes fall on a world made more holy by these deranged days, and in the meantime, may your soul be fed by wolf song and the sound of waves; the land, waters, and skyscapes remind us nothing ever really ends, and you are a breathing once-upon-a-time. A good story is always born in the dark, and here, we sit in the womb of the world. Here, we keep wild.

## 12.4. The Broken Clock
*To Invite the Ease of Timelessness*

Oh, these are the 'twixt and 'tween hours I used to know so well. In my wiser visions, I see the holy hag who lives inside the stars. I hear her celestial resonance echo in my late-afternoon daydreams, and I feel my old names being eclipsed by timelessness, by a birth song of initiation written just for me by that old celestial crone. When she hums, the anxious second hand disappears. When she drums, the weary minute hand twists and spirals like a snake hatchling. Lost in her song, every hour hand on every clock ceases its dance and points west to the land of the dead, reminding us to live as slowly as we can, for as long as the living world will have us.

## 12.5. My More Sullen Hours
*For the Midwinter of the Witch's Soul*

Deep in the midwinter of my Witch's soul, I found myself wandering through a summer dreamscape. The day was hard, sleep took me early, and my dreaming self was swollen with sorrow. There, amidst the sunflowers, a warm, breathy wind from the south struck me and whispered words of contempt. *Remember how short this life is, Witch,* the wind said. *How fleeting is your flesh! Let no more hours be wasted in joylessness. Let no more of your days be sacrificed at the feet of a hungry king who will never learn your name.* The flowers dropped their golden petals then, each taken swiftly by that sharp-tongued southern wind, and I woke with a morning prayer caught in my throat: *May I live well, this day and every day. May my wise and future self bear witness to my most grateful moments here, in the time of my innocence, and may I shed the scaly skin left dead by my more sullen hours.*

## 12.6. Where No Cage Can Hold Me
*Prayer of the Newborn Shape-Shifter*

Tonight, I am shape-shifting into a form that lives closer to what I love. I crawl low on the ground in embodied devotion to this crystal-boned god we call Earth. Tasting ice and mud on my creaturely tongue, I rise to all fours and nuzzle innocence like a newborn fawn. Full of wildness and long-vision, I spread my hairy wings and screech-sing a prayer to the vastness of open skies, to the place where no clock can find me, where no cage can hold me.

## 12.7. Beware the Beauties and the Beasts
*In Honor of the Witch's Imagination*

A Witch's imagination is a dangerous place for a crumbling system. Should a power-thirsty king lose his map and misstep, finding himself on these lawless and overgrown grounds, the wolf-women might just rid him of his blood and breath. Should a false prophet get drunk on his own ego and slip on the rocks of these forbidden shores, the selkies might just drag him beneath the waves and tether his arrogance to the kelp trees. "Beware the beauties and the beasts of this place," we might tell those who dare to visit. "Both will kill any breathing threat to their dream of a wilder world for the wildest children."

## 12.8. The Certainty of Uncertainty
*To Guard Against Duality's Poison*

Some say it is human to perceive the world in terms of opposites. Every this is a not-that, and in the worst of times, our very identities and entire belief systems become bound to — even dependent upon — what they oppose. In this way, the anti-belief empowers the original belief, the very thought it sought to oppose.

Witches and mystics understand the power of consciously holding the tension between two apparently opposing poles, of refusing to surrender to duality and being resourced by the generative fusion of this and that; such practice goes beyond not choosing sides and is not a path for the apathetic. Where duality wishes us to choose between this or that, apathy beckons us toward neither this nor that.

Fertile uncertainty calls us to hold this and that at once and to find the energetic pulse within that tension. Of course, we do not live in a world where we can always operate in the tension, but there is often extreme value in loosening duality's grip on our perception. This is the place in the plot where the trickster meets the innocent, where breaking through the limits of our patterning permits new possibilities to emerge and take shape.

That relentless beast called uncertainty was haunting my dreams, and I picked at a fraying indigo thread called tenderness sprouting from the soft and spoiled place at the edge of my heart. With all the patience of a weaver woman, I wound the thread between my fingers and crooned lost hymns about the most bittersweet of symphonies. I had faith. I took care. I wrapped the thread around my wrists and prayed to the innocent I used to be. I knotted the finest lace around my belly and petitioned my inner scholar to mine the gems of truth from the caverns of confusion. I snarled. I wove that indigo thread through and between my eyes, between each and every tooth, and I hemmed my storyteller's tongue to match my mood. Slowly, surely, I wove an armor to guard against duality's poison, and in time, I heard that once-rotten drum I call heart start beating again, reminding me through its haunted rhythm to always search for the hidden third road.

### 12.9. She Is Bones and Honey
*To the Pilgrim Who Wants a Wild Woman*

Tell me, pilgrim: Do you really wish for a wild woman? Here you are again, waiting on this beach like a lonely fisherman hoping to find a selkie and swipe her pelt, but do you really want a life full of cryptic songs, longing, and sea-salt tears? She'll drag you into the dusk, night after night. She'll steal your sleep and hide it between her legs until you can unlock her midnight secrets. She's a shape-shifter, you know. She's a sea hag with sagging skin and a lustrous beauty made of milk. She is bones and honey, blade and vessel. She'll slip through your fingers like rainwater and return to haunt your bed. So, tell me, do you really wish for a wild woman?

### 12.10. Now, I Keep My Pelt Close
*Lament of the Aging Fox-Woman*

In the days of my youth, I used to bare my wild to anyone who cared to look. Now, I keep my pelt close. I used to hang my heathen skin on the walls of fools and wait for their devotion. I used to drag my beauty through the streets and give my dreams away free of charge. Now, I tend my own den. When a wild king comes sniffing around my door, I ask them if their mother was a shape-shifter and wait. When a mischievous trickster knocks on the walls of my vixen heart, I side-eye their gift, lick their wound, and vanish into the night. Were I to pray to my younger self, I'd petition her to walk with care, to be cautious on the road and keep her soulful pelt tucked away for those who dream of her. I'd say the lovers are many, but the partners are few; both make for good poetry, but it's the latter who can see the medicine in your wild skin.

## 12.11. The Selkie's Pelt
### *A Prayer-Story for the Creaturely Self*

They say a lonely woman can shed three tears into the sea to call a selkie lover toward her, but in many of the old Celtic stories, a human man must steal the pelt of a selkie-woman if he is to keep her. The wild pelt is a common symbol in fairy tales, as the shape-shifter's greatest treasure and liability. Within the wild pelt we see how the gift is also the wound, how our heathen, creaturely nature can be compromised and leave us trapped in someone else's dream.

We also find the hard choices the shape-shifter makes housed in this old Celtic story. If a shape-shifter is always moving closer to what they love, closer to their deep soul, it means leaving lovers and homes behind. It means keeping the pelt close and letting innocence be your teacher. As you read this story, consider what befriending the untamed nature really means in our modern world. What is your wild skin made from, and where do you tuck it away to keep it safe?

Our tale begins like all the best stories do, with a lonely fisherman and a haunting question. In this moment, name your most unanswerable question. Whisper a query aloud that feels like the most pressing question of your life. Maybe the answer will come, maybe it won't, but for now, it is only a question.

Our story begins with that question and a lonely fisherman.

Long ago, in those days of wildness and wonder, a lonely fisherman rowed westward in search of the Otherworld. He was in a rare mood, this haggard creature. You see, this seemingly ordinary morning was, in fact, the solstice of summer, the longest day, the shortest night, a holy time indeed.

Any other year, and this fisherman might not have considered the ancient sanctity of this day, but this year he'd just lived through a quite bizarre Beltane. He had yet to recover from that wild May Day, so in order for me to tell you of this fisherman's solstice, I must first tell you of his Beltane.

They say the Fae will speak to you on Beltane if you let them. They say the merrows, the ondines, and the kelpies will sit in the shadows and keep watch while the humans pretend they rule the world, and then just when those peculiar animals least expect it, those elementals, those tricksters, those spirits of the water, will whisper your real names, the ones only the mist dwellers can pronounce.

They say the veil is thin on Beltane, but it's not that Samhain veil between the living and the dead. No, it's that other, thicker boundary between the human and the more-than-human. Maybe, long ago in the time of his innocence, the fisherman would have remembered these otherworldly wisdoms, but now his voice had begun drying out from having no one to speak to and his heart had been gripped with a tragic bitterness that rid him of all wonder and joy.

So, this fisherman forgot the holiness of Beltane, but sometimes there is a magick in the forgetting. Sometimes we forget so we might remember at just the right time.

On that Beltane morning, nested not so sweetly between the spring equinox and summer solstice, the fisherman woke as he always did, ate some porridge, had a little why-me moment — but then, just then, just before he began dragging his boat over the stones to the sea, he remembered his dream. Now, you know this, but he did not: There are those dreams that house lessons, dreams that mark you, dreams sent straight from the imaginal realms. There are those dreams, and then there are the dreams that feel like prophecy, that have something to say about your fate in this world.

This was the sort of dream the fisherman had that Beltane eve, on the Witches' Night. He dreamt of a seal, but not just any seal. He dreamt of a mystical seal that held the power of prophecy, and he dreamt of his long-dead great-grandfather showing him this creature and telling him of its ways. If you looked in the seal's right eye, his great-grandfather told him in the dreaming time, you saw the most terrible moment of your life. If you looked in the left eye, you saw the most joyful moment of your life. If you looked into one eye, you had to look into the other; this was an otherworldly rule that could never be broken.

"But don't look until you're ready," his great-grandfather warned in the fisherman's dream. "You can't unsee what you see in the eyes of the seal."

That Beltane morning, he remembered this dream while he was dragging his boat to the sea, noticing the precise place where his great-grandfather had stood on the beach. As often happens with telling dreams, he remembered, and then he forgot, spending the whole of the day immersed in his own loneliness.

An initiatory dream always returns for us, though, and just before sunset, just when the fisherman was hauling his nets in, a lone seal popped her little head up from beside his boat. The fisherman was so startled by the creature, he almost fell over, but the little seal stayed right where she was, staring hard at the fisherman with her black-mirror eyes.

Now, the fisherman remembered what his great-grandfather said — don't look until you're ready — and he wasn't at all ready to see what he might behold in the seal's eyes. Instead, he stared at the tip of the little seal's nose. As he did, the claws of loneliness retracted a bit from his heart. He breathed a little easier, and as the sun sank low in the west, he began speaking to the seal.

At first, he just shared a few tidbits about his life. He told the seal how he cooks his porridge and what his favorite work song was, but before he knew it, it was dark, and he was still speaking to this seal. Now, he was telling this seal some deep secrets about his mother and his grandmothers. He didn't know why, but it had been so long since he'd spoken to anyone and the words were just spilling from his mouth like a suddenly undammed river.

Sometimes we tell ourselves we don't have much to say, and sometimes we're right, but sometimes, *sometimes*, we have quite a bit to say and just no one to say it to.

This was how this fisherman's Beltane passed, and every day since that fateful cross-quarter day, the fisherman found himself spilling his secrets to the seal. That seal became his best friend. They shared fish, story, and song. Every day the seal visited. The days grew longer, and the fisherman stayed out on the sea for hours and hours. All the while, he was careful to stare at the tip of her nose. He didn't dare look into her eyes, not yet.

But there was something about today. There was something about this strange summer solstice. Though he had not had any telling dreams since his great-grandfather visited him on Beltane eve, he dreamt of the old man the night before. In this new dream, his great-grandfather stood on the beach and simply said, "Today's the day."

The fisherman woke knowing he was ready. Today was the day. He was going to look in that seal's eyes. *Today's the day.*

So, for all these reasons, the fisherman was in a mood. He paddled past the waves, cast his nets, and waited like he'd done these past few weeks, but on this day, the seal did not come. There was no little gray head poking above the black water. There was no creature there to listen. He stayed brave for a time. He watched the sun in its most beastly form break through the mist. He listened to the gulls, and he waited. And he waited. And he waited.

Around midafternoon he began to lament not looking in the eyes of the seal sooner. It started there, with a small regret, but then he spiraled. He lamented not looking in the eyes of the seal, and then not having children, and then never finding a wife, and then never leaving these lands to which he was born, and then, lastly, sadly, he lamented ever having been born at all.

This is a desperate place, we know — a savage place, really — but it is, importantly, the precise place where the Otherworld sometimes finds us. So in that desperate moment when all hope was lost, the wind went still. The gulls went quiet.

Here, maybe, just maybe, time stopped altogether.

A solstice is a point of pause, you know. A stopping place. It was at this solstice moment when the fisherman heard the song, a song that set his watery world on fire, the song of the selkies. It drifted toward him on an eastward wind, this song about summer and sweetness, this song that filled up his dark and empty places. That song was a seed planted right in his heart, right at that moment, and he couldn't help but move toward that sound.

The singing grew louder, and the fisherman paddled faster, and the sun grew brighter, and then … he saw them, these shape-shifters. Dozens of selkies, all bare-breasted and singing, some with their pelts pulled low and others with their pelts stripped off altogether, some lounging on the rocks in the sun and others diving into the water and laughing. The fisherman had never seen a sight like this, even in his dreams, and he was intoxicated by this moment. He was struck by a mythic beauty his soul somehow remembered, and he wept.

He wept with a wild longing. He was a living spell of grief meeting gratitude, and he wept. The longer you can hold that tension of grief meeting gratitude — the longer you can hold that ache within the ache — the more majestic life becomes. So he watched. He wept, and he became someone new.

*I am marked by this*, he thought. *I am here, and I am not here. I am in the place I've dreamt of, or perhaps this place, these creatures, is dreaming me into being. I am an aching animal made of mist and a quiet god. I am a living ghost.*

These would have been his thoughts if he could have thoughts.

Now, remember, it was the longest day of the year, so you can imagine how long the fisherman was there watching the selkies swim and sing and splash. It was nearly sunset, and he had been there for hours and hours. Slowly, one by one, the selkies were pulling on their sealskins and swimming away. With every selkie that leaped into the water and left, with every inch the sun sank lower on the horizon, the fisherman started to lean away from gratitude and toward grief.

He paddled closer to the rocks now. Only three selkies were left, and then two, and then one.

Now, the fisherman didn't remember how he knew this. Maybe all fishermen simply know the ways of the selkie, or maybe his grandmother told him, or maybe he dreamt it — he wasn't sure — but he knew that if he stole the pelt of a selkie, she must return home with him. He knew this. And there was one selkie left. He thought of his empty house, and there was one selkie left. He thought of his sad, gray mornings, and there was one selkie left.

Now, the pelt was resting on the rocks. The fisherman was so close. He could reach out and swipe it. The selkie was staring eastward at the land, her back to him. All of this happened at once then:

The selkie turned to face him; he looked in her eyes. In her right eye, he saw himself alone and weeping on a beach, his beach. He saw himself shake with a grief he had not yet known. In her left eye, he saw the two of them wrapped together in love, a dark-haired child between them, and he knew now in this moment that he could leave, he could go home, and neither of these moments would come to pass.

He could leave this place, and the best and worst moments of his life would fade into the mist. He knew this. What he didn't know was that the selkie was struck by what she saw in his eyes. In the fisherman's right eye, she saw herself dry, blind, and half-dead, staring seaward from a stony shore. In his left eye, she saw the dark-haired child smiling, holding her sealskin.

She saw great joy and great sadness in the blue eyes of the fisherman, and the two of them lived an entire lifetime just there, the solstice sun setting behind them, the naked selkie looking over her shoulder at the lonely fisherman, and then he reached his hand, so slowly, toward the sealskin, and she saw him do it.

There was a poetry in this moment. He reached for her pelt, she saw him do it, and he tucked it under his coat. She moved toward him, and they both knew this moment couldn't be undone. The severance had happened. There was now *before* this moment and *after* this moment. Before this, the fisherman was adrift on the sea of his life. After this, he'd become bold. Before this, the selkie was an immortal shape-shifter who knew how much of her endless life would unfold. After this, her story was set on another path entirely.

"You will be my wife," the fisherman said or asked or said.

"Yes," the selkie conceded or agreed or conceded.

"In seven years' time, I'll return your pelt to you," the fisherman promised or lied or promised.

What we do know is that the other selkies mourned for her. They watched their shape-shifting sister step into the boat and move toward the shore, and they mourned, these seal-women. They sank beneath the waves and howled. At the same time, the great-grandmother seal, who had seen such things before, lifted her great head over the gray water and watched her wayward daughter sail landward.

For a time, it seemed like it might just be a great love story. The selkie and the fisherman enjoyed each other's company. They shared each other's flesh, and they grew a little more whole together. They had a dark-haired child in time, and they spent simple days that became simple months that became simple years together.

But soon, on the sixth anniversary of their sacred encounter, the selkie's skin began to grow very dry. Her eyesight started to leave her by autumn. By winter, her left arm ached, and by the seventh Beltane after they had met for the first time, the selkie was a pale reflection of who she once was. She spent her days staring at the sea and humming softly to herself. She spent her nights dreaming of her home, of her life underwater.

The selkie was drying out. Their son, little Ronan, noticed his mother's melancholy and wished with all that he was that he could heal her. He wished he could make her whole. He wished harder than he'd ever wished for anything that his mother would be happy.

Ronan wanted his mother to be happy, his parents to stop fighting. One night, their argument was so fierce, he crept out of his window and started running toward the sea. He could still hear his father's voice booming over the hills as he ran.

"You'll leave me if I return your pelt, woman! I know you!"

And his mother's weaker voice: "I must return to what I am. You have not just stolen my skin. You have stolen my home, my soul, all that I am."

"You would leave us. I know you, woman. You are wicked."

The little boy listened, holding his breath, and heard his mother say lastly: "But I'm not a woman, and you don't know me."

Ronan wept for his mother and for his father. He wept with the knowing that they couldn't be together as they once were, and he wept as only a child can weep in the name of their mother.

Maybe it was only in his weeping that he could hear it, just like it was only in his father's lament that he could hear the songs of the selkies so many years ago. But in Ronan's weeping, he heard the voice of his seal aunts, his mother's sisters.

"Ronan, Ronan."

. He couldn't see them, but he could feel them, and he could hear those seal-women when they told him where to look for the pelt. He received their direction as a knowing. He simply knew where to find his mother's pelt.

It was right where the selkie sisters said it was, too, and it smelled so much of his mother that little Ronan sat and nuzzled it for a time. Now in this moment, the choice was Ronan's. He could leave the pelt where it was and his mother would stay, or he could return it to her and his mother would be whole. It was a choice, but it wasn't a choice.

Ronan ran toward the house, but his mother was already stumbling toward the sea. They met, and she saw her pelt. She was met by the precise joyful vision she saw in the fisherman's eye seven years before, and she cried out in an ecstasy only the resurrected understand.

Slipping her pelt on and swimming with her beloved Ronan out into the dark and deep, the selkie was returned, and the return was sweeter than she could ever have hoped. The return was like being wrapped in warmth and ancestral songs after years spent frozen.

*I am falling into myself*, the selkie thought. *I am meeting the moment of my homecoming. I am salt water belonging and the most ancient birth. I am what wildness dreams of. I am my grandmothers' grandmothers' prayers and my child's dream.*

In this moment, in the moment of her return, the worst moment of the fisherman's life came to pass, and he was shaking with grief on the stony beach, his wife and son gone. He wished he never met her. He wished the last seven years away like the memory of a bad dream, yet he knew he wouldn't trade a single night spent with her for years and years of solitude.

Even now, even as the seventh solstice loomed and he wept on the beach for the loss of his small family, he was warmed by the memory of her song. Even now, in the depths of his grief, he would do it all again.

Some say the fisherman remained there on the beach for seven nights, not eating, drinking what rain fell onto his lips. Some say it was little Ronan who found his father, fed him, and nursed his broken heart with laughter, flowers, and innocent questions.

We must remember that though he was a child, little Ronan was half otherling, and he would know the medicine his lonely father needed. He would know the stories to tell, and he would know how to find his mother when he needed her, when the land stories grew dull and he needed the secrets of the sea, he would know how to find the shape-shifter who bore him.

They say Ronan grew to be a great healer who met sorrowful women in times of despair. When they shed three tears into the sea, Ronan brought them gifts of story and song.

They say the fisherman's longing kept him alive and that crack in his heart was mended by the mists, but they don't say the selkie never looked back, because maybe she did.

Maybe she did sun herself on the rocks and look to the land, wishing to be warm in her human flesh, in her soft bed with the fisherman, but she knew it couldn't be. She knew she would have dried to dust had she stayed, and she knew her homecoming was the most beauteous moment in her long, long life, a moment she would never have had if she hadn't found that lonely fisherman on that Beltane morning, if she hadn't gotten into his boat that solstice.

Without the severance, there would be no initiation and no return. This is one of the secrets of the sea.

## 12.12. In Your Name
*A Prayer for the Old Grandmother Seal*

We see you, you old grandmother seal who has seen such things before, who has watched while pelts were stolen and women were left to dry out in the tireless winds of doing. We know there is a story shared by the wiser shape-shifters and elder medicine keepers. We hear it while we dream. We listen for the songs of the seal-women when the children are quiet, and we cast our soulful spells in your name.

## 12.13. This Wallower's Hour
*To Enliven Hope*

A weary Witch without a dream, I am. This day is a bright and blooming hibiscus, but I am a cracked thorn half-buried in bonemeal and mud. The brilliance of the sun is so distant now, and I can scarcely hear the songs of hope echoing overhead. I wonder if I can hear the sound of my soul only when I find myself in deep rest. In my lowlier moments, I wonder if my home is in the underworld, though I refuse its mysteries again and again. This wallower's hour, I petition a child sprite to visit me and strike me with that diamond-dust wand called hope. Enchant my dream-poor heart with those honeyed riches of inspiration and grateful memory. I am ready to wrap a bow around my longing and lay it on the roots of this jewel-orange flower of a day. I am ready to crawl from this quiet garden and bid my gloom to bloom. And so it is.

# 13

# THE BOOK OF BONES AND HONEY

*Prayers for the Bittersweetness
of a Most Heathen Life*

*To see our life as a story* does not mean to detach from reality or surrender to a plotline we did not write. Conversely, when we look through the lens of story, we recover a lost autonomy. We honor our discarded parts, pulling them from the side-character shadows and into the light. One of the more troublesome crimes we might commit against the deep self is to strive to be one pure character who aims only for utter perfection. A heathen story is set within the untamed fringes where the wilds meet modernity, and here, we find ourselves full of sorrow and joy, memory and vision.

We could never be any single one of these archetypes, these "original forms" honored in this heathen prayer book. Our expansive soul would never fit into even these vast spaces of meaning. There are times in our lives when we find more potent archetypal medicine within one form over the others, for certain, but the bittersweetness of our lives demands we stay open to finding healing, power, and meaning in many shapes. Were we to be the warrioress at all times, from birth to death, we would always be striving, protecting, and fighting. We would miss the lover's way of seeing splendor in the small places and the bone-witch's bounty of mourning well. If we were solely a visionary, we would rob ourselves of medicinal presence.

Archetypes are not human; they are energies, and we are not meant to be flesh-and-bone houses for these fluid powers. Archetypes want to move, dance, and breathe. Archetypes are not human, but they are alive, fed by the stories that are told and animate their spirits, that spark them into being with a once-upon-a-time and send them on their way with a happily-ever-after. Like an earthbound ghost, they may refuse to leave and haunt us for a time, but they will not stay forever.

Archetypes show us there are innumerable ways to be, think, and grow. Archetypes can raise temples, start wars, heal lands, and usher in a new age. The more heathen and whole archetypes — those energies that would not get elected or amass millions of followers — will walk with us as we seek out the third road, the tension between *this* and *that*, the hidden option that our dominant, loudest parts will never see.

The prayers contained in this last book, The Book of Bones and Honey, are spoken by a yet-to-be version of you who, strangely, on some timeline, already exists. They wander through a timeless cemetery where wildflowers grow, pondering the merit of these times and their soul's peculiar choice to be here for this, our shared moment. These prayers are yours.

## 13.1. Bones from the Ground and Honey from the Hive
### *When Eco-Depression Comes Creeping*

Tonight, this Witch wanders through a boneyard where the worn graves have no names, where forgotten stories lie silent and unmet longings are food for the worms. I come here to pray, these dire days when whispers of human extinction haunt my joy. On the edge of this unkempt cemetery, a lone hive buzzes with life and drips with heathen honey. A grandmother sycamore reaches her endless arms into the moss, and ghosts walk flanked by howling coyotes. A holier land than this I have not known. I wonder here, as I gather my will like bones from the ground and honey from the hive, if this chapter in the human story might end like a good dream ends, with a narrow escape and timely resolution, or if the end might match those tragic dreams destined to repeat, those telling nightmares where hope is hunted but never found.

All I know for sure, this day, is that the greatest stories are born in the dark, and even the best dreams house crisis.

## 13.2. Where the Old Ghosts Roam
### *To Sing into the Night*

My lantern is dimming, and this moonless night is thick with spirits. Every memory that meets me here on this wild path — every errant thought and every peculiar vision that finds me while I journey home — might be given to me by a ghost. My younger self would be frightened here in this place where the dead walk heavier than the living, but I know better. I know the places where the old ghosts roam are hallowed ground, and I'll sing a solemn song of reverence now as the light dies all around me. I'll bid my ancestors hasten my pace, and I'll find myself home swiftly and safely, my hard edges softened by these otherworldly encounters, my heart full of gratitude that I can see in the dark.

## 13.3. The Underworld's Inkwell
### *When Art Is All There Is*

When the ache is great, we must make art, whatever our art may be. To create intentionally is the great gift of being human, and to live a life devoid of art is to bear the heaviest burden, to carry the raw weight of every unsolved mystery, every incomplete initiation, and every unnamable tragedy. To make art is not to answer every question or heal every wound but to give great meaning to both. In these times, this is our prayer.

An ache finds me now, as the news of the world comes only in colors of red, and I'm calling this timely and tragic ache my muse. Just for today, just because my teeth are worn from the gnashing and my nails are bitten raw, I'm making a peculiar art from my persistent heartbreak. I'm dipping my brush into the underworld's inkwell and tracing the outline of my tears as they drip and slip on the canvas. Each mark is a sigil wept for plastic islands and ghost-tree forests. This art is mine and not mine, as the canvas cocoons itself inside my nightmare. These tears are mine and not mine, as the painting emerges from the husk, spreads its black fur wings, and becomes a devil's door. Lost in the making, I am. Heartbroken by the taking, I found myself this day, yet now I am the living ghost of every sculpture broken by the crafter's hand in a fit of despair. I am the spirit of every half-written book burned in a tumultuous spell of destruction and regret, and I am eco-grief embodied in the soft skin of a world-weary woman.

### 13.4. Love, Innocence, and Climate Crisis
*A Prayer for Young Families*

An extraordinary moment this is. Our strange souls chose each other to share a home in this time of the great unraveling, in these wild moments of war, heat, disease, and rising waters. Fools might call it coincidence, the coming together of our peculiar family, but the knowing ones understand the nature of fate. I vow to see the innocence in you even when fear looms large. I will witness the exquisite beauty of our shared love even when I require solitude, and I will tend this family with the greatest care. May the older-than-ancient gods keep us safe.

### 13.5. For the Love of Bark and Berry
*To Eulogize a Fallen Tree*

Never did I learn your name, my fallen sister. Even so, I weep for you now like a doe over her hunted fawn. You leave a terrible aching absence behind, for with you dies the dream of a land left wild. Even so, if I listen close, I hear the buzz-and-slither songs of life teeming inside the rot. Like a dream left for dead, you are compost for a new and peculiar hope. The longer I stay here, leaving gifts of spit and tears on your flaking bark, the more I am marked by wonder. The more I hear the hymns of your fungal heart, the more I understand the meaning of renewal. Never did I learn your name, but just for today, I will call you my Pagan queen and worship your memory. You house every story ever spoken by the forest dwellers inside your broken roots, and I'll stay right here until I remember who I really am underneath this scarred skin.

### 13.6. These Haunted Evergreens
*To Celebrate What Endures*

So ephemeral is this human life, but the memories of these trees are long. Just now, I find great joy in the soft dance of these knowing evergreens. I find a heathen homecoming in the bounce of their branches, and I celebrate their quiet vitality. They were rooted here before my birth and shall endure long after my death. When that last breath leaves my body, my ghost will visit here in those quiet hours that follow, I think, for my soul will surely remember this moment when I found a fantastic elation in the wind meeting the pines.

### 13.7. The Age of Rot and Renewal
*A Prayer to See the Deep Soul's Vision*

If an initiatory journey is marked by severance, void, and renewal, we might say there are large portions of the collective who are lost in the caves of liminality, who are Inanna on the meat hook in the underworld or the handless maiden wandering through the dark forest. Until the return can occur, until the light of renewal can find us, we are tasked with a time of suspension. Only here can we see the visions the soul needs us to witness. Only here, in the 'twixt and 'tween, can we learn what we must learn.

May we hold our hearts tenderly, in these times of torment. May we trust our souls' intelligence and remember we were sent here by the Fates to be just so, just here, just now. Housed inside our flesh-and-bone home is an alien star seed that we might name teacher in our most sorrowful moments, a treasure gifted us by our future selves to light the way forward, to orient us on our path to tomorrow. If we dare look, we just might find that wily thing called hope shining there like a small sun. If we care to listen, we just might hear the sound of our deep soul's voice inside this golden gift, and should we venture to sit at the feet of that star seed, we will surely humble ourselves before our own genius, becoming dedicant to our holiest purpose here, in the age of rot and renewal.

## 13.8. Licked by 10,001 Forked Tongues
*To Remember When the News Is of Flood and Fire*

When tales of great fires and floods come to the door, may we remember this story we are living is not only written by many hands but stamped by millions of paw prints and licked by 10,001 forked tongues. Our shared story is whipped by a billion wild wings and kissed by a trillion specks of red-rock dust. Moss grows through holes in our happily-ever-afters, and if we put down our pens for a moment, we may just hear the answers to our most pressing questions in the roaring of the flames and the pouring of the rains.

## 13.9. The Strangest Futures
*For Those Who Walk the Third Road*

May we remember the rough way to the hidden third road, these unrestful hours when our twin choices seem to be for *this* or *that*. Here, we find solace in the midnight tension between opposites and curl up to sleep inside the womb of paradox. These are shadow-filled times, and we must be wary of the routes lit so brightly by our screens. We must ask: *Who pointed that spotlight there?* then head into the dark carrying the weight of uncertainty. Fools might name such work apathy, while the wiser ones stay quiet and hone their night vision. An intelligence is afoot here, and we sense the Otherworld's participation in our evolution; we hear the voice of the wild unseen in the spaces between quick decisions. On the third road, we stay open. We stay creaturely, and we pray to the strangest futures we can imagine.

## 13.10. Eco-Spells of Presence
*When a Willow Holds the Only Medicine*

Last night, I pressed my cheek against the bark of a willow and lamented the world I thought I might meet in the years of my wisdom. Surely, I once thought, when time starts to tug at my skin, we will have an antidote for the poisons that sucked the joy from my parents' days. Surely, when the autumn of my life begins to haunt my youth, I will wake in a world without war. The willow whispered words of comfort then, bidding I find sanctuary in these small moments of solitude, in these eco-spells of presence that enchant my soul toward silence.

## 13.11. Slow-Stitching the Birth Tear
### *A Heathen Midwife's Work Song*

The healthiest worlds are the hardest to birth, the heathen midwife knows. Tonight, she stitches the torn flesh of the Earth mother, the wild planet who kept the human soul warm in the womb waters of her seas until it was time for us to slither ashore and stand. Her needle is sharp, but the skin is stone. The labor was rough, and the mother's lifeblood runs in rivers away from the soul of the world. Even so, she stitches swiftly and hums a healing hymn. The midwife's work song is full of a lilting care that eludes the mother's more ungrateful children, but the wiser Witches encircle the birthing bed. Before midnight comes creeping, I shall pray to her, this knowing Witch who speaks the language of life and death. Tell the mother her babe is ailing but healing, I say. Live, live, live, I pray.

## 13.12. The Stubborn Treasure
### *A Prayer for Renewal from the Void*

In my most initiatory moments when that fickle shell that holds my world together flakes and falls away, I become bone-witch and walk through snowdrifts full of snakeskin. I blink the ash from my eyes and look for the bones that remain. I wander through miles of dust and muck to find one splintered stick of ivory that nudges me an inch closer to renewal. I crawl through gray streams thick with the wet cinders of my own undoing, and I dig in deep sloughs for a single remnant, for a stubborn treasure that can never burn.

### 13.13. A Most Heathen Life
*An Ode to the Hive*

At long last, I've found the honey-full hive that hides on the edges of my joylessness. When the old ghosts come creeping and summer's dawn is a million years from this, my coldest midnight, I go to the hive to pray. I kneel at the roots of the hollow tree and commune with the buzzing gods. I weep in reverence to a shining gold future I may never see, and I curl up to sleep inside the shadows of my ancestral dreaming time. My lullaby is the queen's purr, and my restful tonic is a sweet and otherworldly syrup on my tongue. Here, I am in awe of these times, stunned into sleep by the hidden intelligence that made this moment, that nested both me and bee right here, caught between doom and dream, full of a most heathen life.

# CONCLUSION

## *The Witch Maker's Honey*

*Poetry and prayer are the twin languages* of these times. When we leave the patterns of ordinary speech broken, we invite the Other-world to come closer and sing through the spaces between words. In this way, a poet becomes seer. They find a prophecy in the tear-blurred ink of a line they wrote lifetimes ago. They sense a softly stepping ghost haunting a phrase they cannot recall writing, or they notice a visionary gift wrapped inside a single word and left right there, tucked within the faded pages of a forgotten journal. In tune with their muse, a poet is a humble prophet, and poetry becomes prayer to the yet-to-be self, to the soon-to-come world.

In this, the Aquarian age of unprecedented technological evolution, we might wonder what will become of poetry. If an artificially intelligent program can produce a lyric that passes as art, what motivation will drive the young poets to sit in the discomfort of their angst and write? What if software learns how to sing in ways that stir the soul, and what meaning will our art hold if it is brewed outside the dark womb of human longing? Those of us who claim — or dance around the reclamation of — the name heathen, who dare to remember the many troubled and interwoven histories of that word, might wonder if the new colonizer creeping from the shadows is inhuman.

An inescapable modern debate, one that has been used for centuries to tether laws to women's bodies, focuses on the moment life begins. Does a human soul spark to life at conception, the quickening, birth, or somewhere in between? We may also ask: At what point does art come alive? Does a painting live when the artist dreams of it, dips the brush, paints the first stroke, weeps the first frustrated tear, or finally hangs it on a wall after months or years of gestation? Whatever the answer, we may also ask, is art instantaneously produced by AI conceived at all, or is it merely a stillborn mimicry of the human creative impulse to manifest the imagined?

These are the trickster's questions. If nothing new can be born without the wily hand of the trickster midwife, then perhaps AI is more coyote than colonizer. Perhaps these are the early days of the apocalypse science-fiction writers, as witting or unwitting prophets themselves, have predicted in novels and film for decades, and maybe to be heathen not only means to live on ground untamed by the church or imperialism but to make art there on that wild heath where human wounds bleed onto the canvas, where no algorithm dare tread, where aching souls risk death for a taste of that heathen-honey muse, and where songs of longing are stung onto the tongue.

We might wonder if this is the moment when humanity unites against a new virus, one we ourselves created and taught how to adapt to any vaccine we might wield against it, one that threatens not the flesh but the very soul of the world. When the nourishing work of creation is tasked to technology, surely all human meaning will be lost to memory. Surely prayer will not be sufficient in guarding against a new unseen intelligence, one not otherworldly but, by contrast, immune to the Otherworld's necessary participation in any creative act.

Every Witch, maker, and artist knows the muse enters in from the fringes. Every piece of art has been kissed by the mythic. We don't know how it happens, and we aren't meant to. The maker wonders if the world unfolds inside art first before manifesting in the material, before animating world events or shaping the next chapter in the world story. What if this otherworldly muse we cannot name is always calling us forward and trying to orient us toward collective healing? What if art is not a clear mirror that reflects but a black mirror that predicts? With AI writing new scripts sourced only from old uploaded ideas, art becomes devoid of the muse's voice, a wasteland where the Otherworld finds no home, where the whispers of the wise and future self cannot be heard.

The trickster might wonder, though, whether inhuman art may not be the end of us but a new beginning, an unexpected once-upon-a-time that ushers in an unprecedented wave of the wildest human-born creative work ever imagined. How attuned to the muse will a human artist have to be in order to outwit and outshine AI? What if, driven by an unnamable need to retain its most integral and original purpose, humanity evolves into its most ingeniously expressive form, a species so imaginative it could not only save the planet but give birth to a new age where art is currency.

A heathen lives close to the Earth and close to the soul. So wary are they of any outside force that might fence in their freedom, and their prayers are not for a return to the days when childbirth often meant death and lives depended wholly on the fertility of the fields. The prayers of the modern heathen are for a good life followed by a good death, for an Earth-conscious future to unfold for humanity after their flesh feeds the ground. To that end, the heathen stays attuned to the Otherworld, intentionally finding moments of stillness and presence where the yet-to-be might sing to them, where the Holy Wild reminds them why they were born here and now.

## A Heathen Seed: A Final Prayer-Story

Once in a time that was always and never, the last free poet stared seaward at a looming storm. Her Earth was full of wildfires, ghost-tree forests, and fallow soil swollen with salt and stunted human dreams. She prayed to her lost ancestors who live as we live to keep her hidden for another hour, to protect her from the art-hungry programs in power who devoured human poetry like food.

No one remembered when the software began breathing, but some say it was after the last story was bitten by technology's teeth, after the last painting was digested and retched back onto a screen. All say it was before the artists were captured, caged, and bred to be the most creatively fertile creatures ever born. In a silver subterranean forest prison, these human makers live, dance, paint, sing, write, and strive to make sense of a world left wounded by inhuman intentions. Their art sustains the technology. Without the human creative impulse, the programs wither and die.

Today, when her prayers are complete, the last free poet goes to liberate her kin. She bids farewell to her sea-salt home and sets out on the wild road toward the subterranean forest. In her heart, she holds a seed bred of the artists in the underground, a heathen seed called ancestral memory. The prisoner artists have no songs stuck in their marrow by their grandmothers, but the last free poet's bones are full of her forebears' prayers. She sings a song of longing and truth so loudly that the machines will surely hear her and take her into the Great Below, and there she will howl poetry born in a time before time. The artists will lick their cages open with a fork-tongued madness suddenly alive in their blood, and the soulless technologies will starve before dawn, leaving their rusted husks to be crushed under the footfalls of a most liberated humanity, a heathen tribe of creative deviants who remake the world anew.

And so it is.

We can be heathen and still be grateful for the conveniences afforded us by this modern age. Fairy-tale intelligence shows us how we, like our stories, house a wealth of archetypal energies and, by extension, intense contradictions. We can appreciate that social media sometimes saves lives and despise the damage it has done to our psyches. We can fall in love with a solitary screenless wander in the wilderness and be thankful for the app that shows us the way home. We can honor our sovereignty as well as our interrelatedness. In essence, we are the third road. We *are* the energetic tension that arises when opposing forces are contained and held, and this tension is a source not of weakness but of power.

When we befriend our heathen nature, we resist the labels that feel too easy or too pure. There is no perfection in a heathen life. Every day has its dirt. The etymology of *perfection* is "to be finished" or "to go to the end," and the heathen wants to live. Even now, when so many of our hours are marked by a complicated uncertainty, the heathen wants to live and live well. Even now, we pray for simplicity and indulgence, water and mud, gods and godlessness, wisdom and innocence. May we all find the medicine we seek, and on the days we find ourselves beyond prayer, if nothing else, may we remember the troubling majesty of being human.

# ACKNOWLEDGMENTS

*To the hairy potter I call husband,* thank you for cooking for me, our children, and the circles of Witches who come to visit us on the haunted land you tend so well. To Bodhi and Sage, thank you for choosing me as your mother and for choosing to be born in these times. To those whom I have been blessed to call teacher — including Bayo Akomolafe, Sean de Cantuail, and Dr. Clarissa Pinkola Estés — thank you for your immense wisdom, your writings, and your sacred work in the world. To the team at New World Library, including my editor Georgia Hughes and publicist Kim Corbin, and to my agents Sheree Bykofsky and Jill Marsal, the deepest bows and wildest howls for all you have done in midwifing these strange books of mine. To my grandmother Grace, I miss you. Thank you for growing me up from my roots. To the snowy Mohawk land that has claimed me, I say thank you and vow to protect and tend you well.

# NOTES

## The Trickster's Bone Broth: An Introduction

p. 2    *The etymology of* apocalypse: *Online Etymology Dictionary*, s.v. "apocalypse," accessed January 28, 2023, https://www.etymonline.com/word/apocalypse.

p. 3    *The etymology of* archetype: *Online Etymology Dictionary*, s.v. "archetype," accessed January 28, 2023, https://www.etymonline.com/word/archetype.

p. 3    *The word-story origin of* thespian: *Online Etymology Dictionary*, s.v. "thespian," accessed January 28, 2023, https://www.etymonline.com/word/thespian.

p. 4    *The word* prayer, *from the Old French*: *Online Etymology Dictionary*, s.v. "apocalypse," accessed January 28, 2023, https://www.etymonline.com/search?q=prayer.

p. 4    *heathens were "dwellers on the heath"*: *Online Etymology Dictionary*, s.v. "heathen," accessed January 28, 2023, https://www.etymonline.com/search?q=heathen.

p. 7    *the etymology of the word* war: *Online Etymology Dictionary*, s.v. "war," accessed January 28, 2023, https://www.etymonline.com/word/war.

## 4. The Book of the Heathen Queen

p. 55   *In fairy tales, we find*: Marie-Louise von Franz, *The Interpretation of Fairy Tales* (Boulder, CO: Shambhala, 1996).

## 5. The Book of the Moon

p. 63   *The trickster is said to be amoral*: For more information on the trickster archetype, see Lewis Hyde, *Trickster Makes This World* (New York: Farrar, Straus and Giroux, 1998).

p. 67   *"The White Wolf," "Le Loup Blanc," is a French fairy tale*: Auguste Gittée and Jules Lemoine, *Contes populaires du pays wallon* (n.p.: Gand, 1891), 19–23.

## 7. The Book of the Wounded Healer

p. 92   *"Gold Tree and Silver Tree" is a fairy tale*: Joseph Jacobs, *Celtic Fairy Tales* (London: David Nutt, 1892), 252.

## 9. The Book of the Pagan Warrioress

p. 126   *"bleeding keys" we hold to our own hidden darkness*: For a Jungian analysis of this folk tale and the symbolism of the bleeding key, see Dr. Clarissa Pinkola Estés, *Women Who Run with the Wolves* (New York: Random House, 1992).

## 10. The Book of the Botanical Babe

p. 146   *"It is good to be born in a church"*: Swami Vivekananda, *The Complete Works of Swami Vivekananda* (Calcutta, India: Advaita Ashrama, 1989), 400.

## Conclusion: The Witch Maker's Honey

p. 180   *The etymology of* perfection: *Online Etymology Dictionary*, s.v. "perfection," accessed January 28, 2023, https://www.etymonline.com/word /perfection.

# ABOUT THE AUTHOR

*Danielle Dulsky is an Aquarian mischief maker*, painter, and word-witch. Author of *The Holy Wild Grimoire* (New World Library, 2022), *Sacred Hags Oracle* (New World Library, 2021), *Seasons of Moon and Flame* (New World Library, 2020), *The Holy Wild* (New World Library, 2018), and *Woman Most Wild* (New World Library, 2017), Danielle is the founder of The Hag School and believes in the power of wild collectives and sudden circles of curious dreamers, cunning Witches, and rebellious artists in tending to the world's healing. Mother to two wildlings and partner to a potter, Danielle fills her world with nature, family, old stories, and intentional awe. Find her in the haunted wilds of central New York or the whiskey-soaked streets of a Pennsylvania steel town; she calls both places home.

**DanielleDulsky.com**
**TheHagSchool.com**